JOACHIM REMAK, chairman of the department of history at Lewis and Clark College, currently is a visiting associate professor of history at Indiana University. He holds B.A. and M.A. degrees from the University of California at Berkeley and a doctoral degree from Stanford University.

Professor Remak has been on the board of editors of *Documents on German Foreign Policy, 1918-1945,* and his book on the assassination of Archduke Franz Ferdinand, *Sarajevo,* won the Hoover Library Borden Award for 1960. His articles and reviews have been widely published in professional journals and general periodicals including *American Historical Review, Aussenpolitik,* and *Harper's.*

Th. Fontane

the GENTLE CRITIC

THEODOR FONTANE *and*
GERMAN POLITICS, 1848-1898

JOACHIM REMAK

 1964

SYRACUSE UNIVERSITY PRESS

Manufactured in the United States of America.
Composition and printing by The Heffernan Press Inc.,
Worcester, Massachusetts, binding by The Vail-Ballou
Press, Inc., Binghamton, New York.

To Frederick and Virginia Breier
in Friendship

Cold wind filled rooms and hallways
Unlocked were portal and door
When the Brandenburgers buried
Their old squire Otto von Rohr.

Six Rohrs—cousins all—bear the coffin
Six more walk in step with theirs
They are followed by three von der Hagens
And three von Häselers.

A Ribbeck, a Stechow, a Zieten
A Rathenow, a Quast
The coffin's weight grows heavy
As barns and fields move past.

The cemetery sparkles
With autumn's last sunshine
And red is the glow of the barberries
Beneath the dark green of the vine.

The militia flag held by von Bredow
Saw action in eighteen-thirteen
And Hans Rochow von Reckahne
Was the last to join the scene.

THEODOR FONTANE, *"Adlig Begräbnis"*

Old Mrs. Wangenheim always told me (putting on her most Catholic face as she did so), "Prussia-Germany is without promise." That is right. We are not mentioned in the Old Testament. The British act as though they *had* the promise.

THEODOR FONTANE to August von Heyden, August 5, 1893

Preface

THE YEAR 1871 in the history of Germany seems almost more remote to us than the year 1789 in that of France. In many ways, the Franco-Prussian War and the creation of the German Empire belong to a past more strange and distant than the French Revolution. But if remoteness is supposed to bring with it the benefits of historical perspective, it has notably failed to do so in the case of late nineteenth century Germany and Prussia. The period still will not quite come into focus; we still seem to fluctuate between the extremes of sweet nostalgia and bitter recrimination.

In recent years, the latter attitude has predominated. Several writers have seen little but illiberalism, militarism, and racial bigotry—in short, a great rehearsal for National Socialism—in nineteenth century Germany and Prussia. By using some of the more extreme of German writers and politicians as sources and by reinterpreting other less extreme ones they have seen a straight and logical line extending from Bismarck—if not from Frederick the Great or Luther—to Adolf Hitler. Anyone writing a social history of the United States with the plays of Tennessee Williams as his chief source would probably encounter a very skeptical critical reception, but we have recently accepted, with very little scholarly resistance, histories of Germany in which Treitschke has been mentioned at length and Ranke not at all, or in which the anti-Semitic Stoecker has been treated as Germany's most representative nineteenth century Christian theologian.

But if it is patently absurd to present shrill fanatics as the exclusive spokesmen of the German character, if it will profit us little to see Himmler in Moltke or Goebbels in Goethe or Hitler in Wilhelm I, it is plain, too, that some things did go wrong in nineteenth century Germany. Hitler did not suddenly spring into being, full-grown and onto an entirely alien soil, in 1933. Certain defects did plague Bismarck's Reich from its very beginnings.

The time has come—whether we have the discovery of the roots of twentieth century disasters in mind or not— to take a fresh look at that Reich, at the meaning of the term "Prussian," and at German society and thought in the second half of the nineteenth century. The present book is a modest contribution toward such a reconsideration. It deals with how one German critic, the novelist Theodor Fontane, saw matters at the time. Several reasons (a great personal fondness for Fontane as a novelist aside) supported this preoccupation with Fontane as a political critic. For one thing, it seemed useful to contrast some of the more rabid writers, so frequently cited in recent years, with a calmer one who has been cited much more sparingly, even though his German popularity both then and now has been considerable. Moreover, his criticisms show a balance that is rare. Other German critics of their nation's weaknesses, such as Hölderlin, Heine, or Nietzsche, have been far more violent and absolute in their judgments. Fontane's criticism is of a gentler variety, but it is also more objective, more understanding, and perhaps more fruitful. "Maximilian Harden," wrote Fontane of another of the harsher critics, "is very clever, very deft, and very courageous. But stern masters do not govern very long." Fontane was a rather mild master, deceptively mild perhaps, but in any event he made up in common sense whatever he lacked in sternness.

He also was a great artist and a wonderful observer. No one else has described the atmosphere, the manners, and the spirit of *fin de siècle* Berlin and Brandenburg

quite as beautifully and accurately as did Fontane in his
novels and letters. He was a part of the world he wrote
about; he was very fond of it, in fact, and he knew and
appreciated the things which made it pleasant. He could
also step outside it, however, and see its failings with
equal discernment. How then did Fontane judge his
Prussia and his Germany? His answers may be as useful
as any we are capable of offering a century later.

A word about the translations. All passages from Fontane are cited in my own translation. This applies to
poetry as well as to prose. Critics of the former are asked
if not for forebearance at least for charity. To translate
poetry well, and faithfully, is the one task that is even
harder than to arrive at a balanced judgment of nineteenth century Germany.

In other areas, more help was received, and is acknowl-
edged with genuine gratitude. Both Miss Jean McNett
and Mrs. Viola Watson Ndenga of the Lewis and Clark
College Library labored far beyond the call of duty to ob-
tain source material that was as rare and elusive as it was
essential. My cousin and far better Fontane scholar,
Henry H. H. Remak, has aided and advised me on more
than one phase of this work with a generosity which is
easier to note than to repay; he also made available, from
his collection of Fontane manuscripts, the letter, written
in August 1887, from which the signature beneath the
frontispiece has been taken. The Theodor-Fontane-Archiv
in Potsdam, through the kind offices of Bibliothekar
Joachim Schobess, very generously loaned both the Max
Liebermann chalk drawing of Fontane which appears on
the book jacket and the line drawing based on it which
has been used for the frontispiece. Several publishers have
graciously permitted the quotation of copyrighted material: Coward-McCann (A. J. P. Taylor, *The Course of*

German History), G. Grote'sche Verlagsbuchhandlung (Theodor Fontane, *Briefe an die Freunde*), Insel-Verlag (Hugo von Hofmannsthal, "Lebenslied"), Quelle & Meyer (Theodor Fontane, *Briefe an Georg Friedlaender*), and Simon and Schuster (William Shirer, *The Rise and Fall of the Third Reich*).

A special note of appreciation, finally, is due to the Danforth Foundation. A faculty grant given on faith, before the topic had ever taken shape, provided an essential period for research and reflection without which this book might have remained unwritten.

Contents

CHAPTER I

Theodor Fontane's Life

A minor office, a small decoration
A dash of honors to show one's station
A special party at seventy
A daughter who can list a degree
A son in the army and let me see
They once almost bestowed a title on me.
Two encyclopedias abstract the fame:
Both Brockhaus and Meyer list the name.
Old Prussian average—in sum
It was always a matter of hey diddle dum
Of hey diddle dum and dee and such.
All in all: it was not much.

THEODOR FONTANE, *"Summa Summarum"*

THEODOR FONTANE'S LIFE nearly spans the nineteenth century. He was born in the small town and district seat of Neuruppin, some half-dozen miles north of Berlin, in 1819—four years after Bismarck, who throughout Fontane's life was to occupy his imagination as no other man would. Both his parents were descended from French Huguenot as well as from German Protestant ancestors. His father, Louis Henri Fontane, was a pharmacist, owner first of the Löwen-Apotheke in Neuruppin, and then of the Adler-Apotheke in Swinemünde. It was his family's intention that Theodor Fontane should follow the same profession. His education toward this end was somewhat haphazard. He did attend the *Gymnasium* in Neuruppin and later on in Berlin, but formal schooling frequently gave way to his father's rather happy-go-lucky tutoring. The immediate family background can best be described perhaps by reversing the roles of Goethe's

Vom Vater hab' ich die Statur
Des Lebens ernstes Führen,
Vom Mütterchen die Frohnatur,
Die Lust zu fabulieren.

1

It was his mother who was forced to cope with life's seriousness, while his father—a man with little business acumen but a great deal of *joie de vivre*—taught his son the pleasures of a good story well told.

At the age of seventeen, Fontane left school without graduating, to become an apothecary's apprentice. For over a decade, he worked as a pharmacist, with apparent competence, and next to no enthusiasm. His true inclination was to be a writer. His talent here was obvious and had showed itself early. He wrote his first poetry at fourteen, published some ballads when still a pharmacist's apprentice, and in the eighteen forties was invited to join a literary group in Berlin, the *Tunnel über der Spree.* It was a distinguished and convivial company, among whose members were Count Moritz Strachwitz, Theodor Storm, and the future Nobel Prize winner Paul Heyse. In this period, Fontane wrote and published a good deal of poetry, primarily translations of English and Scottish ballads, as well as historical poems of his own, which were to become highly popular, and in which he celebrated the generals of Frederick the Great and other heroes of Prussia's past.

In the eighteen fifties, Fontane sought an escape route from the pharmacist's trade in an equally unsatisfactory excursion into the civil service. The attempt lasted for nearly eight years, a tribute to Fontane's Prussian persistence if not to his abilities as a bureaucrat. Employed by the press section of the Prussian Ministry of the Interior and by similar government agencies, Fontane—imaginative, subtle, restless—never quite made his peace with the rather different milieu characteristic of the Prussian (or any other) civil service.

His changed employment—or, to be more precise, the false hopes which it aroused—did enable him to marry Emilie Rouanet, to whom he had been engaged for some time, and to do a fair amount of traveling. In 1855, he moved to England to be the editor of an Anglo-German news service. The enterprise, despite all the great plans Fontane had for it and despite all the financial support the Prussian government granted it, turned out to be short-lived, and a year later he returned to Berlin. In 1858, he finally left the government service for the most precarious of all careers: that of a professional writer. (It was a step, let it be recalled, which not even Goethe had chosen to take, preferring as he did to earn his living as a working politician throughout his life.) For over a decade, Fontane wrote for the ultra-conservative *Kreuzzeitung*. He covered all three of Prussia's wars for the paper: that against Denmark in 1864, that against Austria in 1866, and that against France in 1870. During that last conflict, he was exposed to more than the customary dangers of a war correspondent. In a trip behind the lines, he was arrested by the French, who held him as a suspected spy, and would release him only upon the personal intercession of Bismarck and of some sympathetic American diplomats. On his return home, he changed over to the more liberal *Vossische Zeitung*, which invited him to become its theater critic. It was with this newspaper that he remained until his retirement nineteen years later, at the age of seventy, in 1889.

His work on both papers left him with a fair amount of time and leisure for his own writing. His first travel book, *Ein Sommer in London,* had appeared in 1854, and he now followed this with a number of other books of travel and reminiscence, including *Jenseits des Tweed* (1860), *Aus England* (1860), *Kriegsgefangen* (1871), and *Aus den Tagen der Okkupation* (1872). All still make rewarding reading, but the greatest of these books is the splendid and unique combination of scenic description, anecdote, and local history, the four-volume *Wanderungen durch die Mark Brandenburg* (1862-1882) with the sequel *Fünf Schlösser* (1889).

In the late eighteen seventies, Fontane—poet, journalist, travel writer, author of popular history—turned to yet another field, that of the novel. The change was not an entirely abrupt one. *Vor dem Sturm* (1878), his first novel, dealt with a historical topic, the eve of the War of Liberation, and *Grete Minde*, published two years later, took its plot from a seventeenth century Brandenburg chronicle. But in the books that followed, he turned to the contemporary world of Berlin bourgeois and Brandenburgian squire, most notably in *L'Adultera* (1882), *Irrungen Wirrungen* (1888), *Stine* (1890), *Frau Jenny Treibel* (1892), *Effi Briest* (1895), and *Der Stechlin* (1899). They are all of them delightful books, characterized by an absence of sentimentality, by gentle irony, and by a penetrating understanding of and sympathy for the people and places they describe. As social documents, they may be without equal, and at least two of them, *Effi Briest* and *Der Stechlin*, are great books. What may be without parallel, too, is this late unfolding of the novelist's talent. Fontane, after all, was nearly sixty when his first novel appeared, and he was to write the best of his novels in his late seventies; the older he grew, the more distinguished his work became. The other famous late talent in German literature, Conrad Ferdinand Meyer, who did not begin to write in earnest until he was approaching forty, appears almost a youth by comparison.

The last two decades of Fontane's life also were among his happiest. He had found his true vocation and a good deal of external success besides, and he felt that he no longer had any need to engage in the mild social climbing of his younger years. To quote the older Theodor Fontane on himself: *"Alles Strampeln abgetan"*[1]—no more fidgeting, no more thrashing about. In 1898, the year in which Bismarck died and *Der Stechlin* was completed, Fontane died in Berlin. His final resting place is a simple grave in the *Französische Kirchhof*, the cemetery of the French community in Berlin.[2]

Fontane, the chronicler of what one is tempted to call for short the "Prussian Establishment" in the nineteenth century, thus both belonged and failed to belong—at least entirely—to the world of the rich, the well-born and the able that he so often wrote about. His qualifications as an insider are many: he was born and raised in the heart of Old Brandenburg; he spent most of his working life in Berlin; many of his closest friends bore aristocratic names; he wrote for both the *Kreuzzeitung*, the organ of the Prussian Tory squire, and for the *Vossische Zeitung*, the paper of the wealthy Liberal bourgeois of Berlin; he was a person of polished manners who had learned to enjoy the parties given by the subscribers of either paper. What makes him something of an outsider is perhaps not quite so obvious. In view of some of the rather foolish things that have been written within recent memory about the German character, let it be emphasized first that it was not his French descent—not in a Prussian society that happily counted among its own an Adalbert von Chamisso, a Friedrich de la Motte-Fouqué, an Ambassador von Pourtalès, a General von François. Besides, for all his father's playing the role of jolly Gascon, his ancestry was German as much as French.

No, it was a class-conscious, not a race-conscious society in which Fontane, the bourgeois, the ex-pharmacist, the unsuccessful civil servant, the self-taught writer who had left the *Gymnasium* short of graduating did not quite fit.

"I remember being present in Saxony," wrote Mme. de Staël earlier in the century, "at a lecture on metaphysics given by a celebrated philosopher who always quoted

Baron Leibniz, and the enthusiasm of his discourse never once induced him to omit this title of baron."[3] Here, as a consequence, Fontane at times felt less than wholly at ease, although given his sensitivity in the matter, he would forestall actual embarrassment by keeping a certain voluntary distance between himself and his aristocratic friends. The more intimate family gatherings of the country gentry, for instance, had better be avoided by social outsiders, he once wrote. "Even now, in my old age, after achieving, through toil and trouble, the highest rank possible to people like me: an encyclopedia entry; even now I studiously absent myself from country weddings, baptisms, and funerals—and funerals are the worst—even where the families of friends are concerned. For one's friends are not in charge on such days, and in place of a mild and pleasant domestic air there suddenly reigns an icy class atmosphere, produced by the sheer mass of the kind of people invited. The two friends, noble and bourgeois, sweat blood and water, while the proponents of a higher social order, usually decked out in the uniforms of their provincial dignities, or at least equipped with the Order of St. John, don't quite know what to make of one. One might seek refuge in wearing one's Order of the Eagle or of the Crown, if one should possess them, but that is risky business, too, since it might be interpreted as a claim to equality, in which case the cost would be greater than the profit. So there you stand with your white tie, which if ill luck will have it will be on a bit crooked, too, and what you read on most faces is: 'Well, I suppose he'll want to write about it,' something which everyone will at one and the same time very much like to see and consider rather low and almost common. That is the way it still is."[4]

Does a certain melancholy hide behind the light touch? Perhaps. But whatever Fontane's social problems were (and they were never tragic in nature, nor did they dominate his life), it is the reader who gains from them. For "write about it" was precisely what he did wish to do, and his personal position made him the ideal chronicler of Brandenburgian country gentry and Berlin society. He was, in short, enough of an insider to describe either group with utter accuracy and enough of an outsider to find their activities intriguing enough to serve him as story material. Writers who are born into aristocracy or into elegance seldom seem to find such interest in their own world. Count Platen, for example, to name one compatriot of Fontane's, channeled most of his energies into Gothic poems. Heinrich von Kleist, to name another, wrote about exotic events in foreign lands, or about peasant pranks, or if he did write about Prussia—and what could be more Prussian than either *The Prince of Homburg* or *Michael Kohlhaas*—he dealt with Prussia's past and not its present. Marcel Proust would seem to be the exception rather than the rule. Had Fontane been born a Baron von Fontane auf Itzenplitz, we might have had no *Effi Briest* and no *Stechlin*.

All in all, it was a great deal, and even the white tie usually was tied very well.

CHAPTER II

Fontane's Politics

> Freedom—of course. But evil looms large
> Wherever the masses are left in charge.
> Even the freest of souls will concede
> The wisdom, the prudence, the utter need
> (Why not admit what we all understand)
> Of clear and firm laws, of the clear,
>   firm command.

THEODOR FONTANE, *"Festes Gesetz"*

CERTAINLY it was not Fontane's political convictions which accounted for any insurmountable barriers between himself and Prussia's Tory squires. True, in his earlier years his sympathies were decidedly Liberal, but so were the young Bismarck's for instance. "A normal product of our government-sponsored education," read the opening lines of Bismarck's memoirs, "I left school at Easter 1832, as a pantheist, and if not as a republican, then with the conviction that a republic was the most reasonable form of government."[1] "All my poetry," wrote Fontane in a similar vein in his memoirs about his youth, "was tuned to the theme of liberty."[2] As usual, he leavened his sentiments with irony: "That liberty had not arrived yet did not make me too acutely unhappy. Perhaps it was even fortunate for me, for else I would not have been able to call for it."[3] But in truth his liberal convictions went deep and evaporated less rapidly than Bismarck's. When 1848 came, Fontane squarely stood on the side of the revolution, and only luck and his sense of the ludicrous may have saved him from prison or exile as the revolution collapsed.

Fontane's own recollections embellish the role he played that year with a touch of comedy that is perhaps

9

just a shade too neat—was not Laurence Sterne's journey, too, funnier in the telling than in the event?—but they give a convincing enough picture of his political sentiments. In the spring of 1848, Fontane wrote many years later, he welcomed the revolution in Berlin with enthusiasm and was more than eager to contribute his share toward its triumph. On March 18, 1848, when troops fired on the crowds and in response the barricades went up, his first thought was to ring the bells and sound the tocsin of revolution. Rushing to the nearest church to do so, he found, to his chagrin, that the doors were locked—"Protestant churches are always closed." No matter, he would break in the door. Looking around for the proper battering ram, he was happy to see a rather shaky wooden pole used for holding up a clothesline. Alas, success once again was to elude him: "like an occasional molar which is shaky, too, and whose staying power one therefore underestimates, the pole would not come out." He went on trying like a man obsessed for several minutes before conceding to the pole, "shooting off my best power against it, as it were, for my strength would not return later. . . . My debut as a ringer of bells in storm warning had failed."

The next morning, however, his strength had returned, and he joined a group of workers in search of arms. The search proved more successful than the attack on the laundry pole, as the crowd broke into the prop room of the Königstädter Theater and grabbed spears, halberds, and muskets. Fontane seized a musket, a firearm of venerable vintage which, by all appearances, had last seen service in musical comedy. He then proceeded to pick up a gloveful of gun powder and joined a crowd that had taken up position behind a barricade constructed of cardboard mountains and canvas forests—the stage scenery, too, had been pressed into the service of the revolution. He still was without bullets, but he thought that coins might serve and so began pouring immense quantities of gunpowder into his stage musket. His activity was interrupted by a Berliner who had been watching him all the while and who, as the barrel was half filled with powder, said rather quietly, "Now, really— *na hören Sie.*" The words, spoken in kindness, not in ridicule, abruptly sobered Fontane who with some shock realized the dubiousness of the weapon which he had proposed to use, and the absurdity of trying to fill it with enough gunpowder to blow up a small mountain. In a subdued but by no means entirely unhappy mood—"dying in battle just for the sake of dying in battle was alien to me"—he withdrew from the impending combat and spent the remainder of the revolution as a spectator rather than as a participant.[4]

Still, the substitution of reflection for action did not imply any repudiation of the revolution. Fontane was pleased when that spring the voters of his district made him an Elector of Delegates to the Frankfurt Assembly.[5] As for those who argued that the country was not yet ready for the work of such an Assembly, that the foundations for democratic government did not exist in Germany, Fontane had this to say to a friend in the autumn of 1848: "My answer is: a good and civilized people is always ready for freedom."[6] Nor did he abandon these convictions as he saw the revolution defeated. When Friedrich Wilhelm IV abruptly refused the Imperial crown offered to him by the Assembly, Fontane was indignant: "The king's answer is so incredible that I wonder—not the king himself, but his doom speaks and acts through him. A *free* man, a king . . . could not speak like that."[7] Later he would be less charitable about the king's motives, quoting the poet Georg Herwegh's angry lines about Friedrich Wilhelm IV with obvious approval:

> Too shy to look the new age in the eye
> Too greedy for applause to treat it with contempt
> And too well-born to comprehend its spirit.[8]

And if, in order to reach the new age, one had to face the threat of mob rule (a prospect which had earlier given Fontane and his friends some pause), one should be ready to accept even that. A change was needed in Prussia, and "mob rule is the bridge across which we must pass."[9]

In subsequent years, however, Fontane's Liberal enthusiasm grew perceptibly weaker. For one thing, Fontane had too subtle and too ironic a mind to accept any party slogan or even program at face value; life appears in the round in his political thought as well as in his novels. A weakness of the revolution which came to strike him with particular force was one he had still denied in 1848: the country was not yet ready for popular government. "All day long," Fontane wrote to his son toward the end of his life, "I watched you sit next to the ballot box—a sight fit for the gods. This whole election business cannot possibly be wisdom's final and most splendid stage. In England or America perhaps, or even certainly—but in Germany, where first a policeman, and then a battalion, and then a battery stand behind every voter, it all seems like a waste of time to me. What must stand behind a popular election is popular sovereignty, and if that is missing, none of the rest matters."[10] And he was only too convinced that it was still missing: "Anyone who wants to make a revolution in Prussia must be very optimistic, frivolous, or *very* brave. That is true even today, despite the Social Democrats."[11]

Despite all these second thoughts, Fontane, unlike

Bismarck, would never ridicule the Liberals. For one thing, the reasons behind the revolution had been too sound. In a passage written nearly half a century after 1848, he cited some of these reasons which, for all his later conservatism, he could see very plainly still. It is a passage which will bear repeating, for it tells us about Fontane the writer, Fontane the political observer, Fontane the historian, and a great deal about the background of 1848 besides.

"Immediately following the February [1848] days, there was ferment everywhere, and Berlin was no exception. One was tired of the old approach to things. Not that one had suffered particularly under it; no, it was not that. It was, rather, that one was ashamed of it.

"If one looked at politics, everything was antiquated, and at that, attempts were being made to bring back things that were even more ancient and to surround this debris with a sort of halo, for the pretense was that one 'wished to serve true freedom and healthy progress.' And in the process, there were constant references to the 'country of ancient wisdom and political continuity.' Yet one had overlooked one minor detail here. It was that England had always known freedom, while Prussia never had. England had grown in the age of Magna Charta; Prussia, in that of flourishing absolutism, in the age of Louis XIV, Charles XII, and Peter the Great. Before our states had been formed or combined, there did exist in individual parts of the country medieval feudal [*ständisch*] constitutions which one now wished to use again with the addition, perhaps, of some new splendors. This, then, so the word went, was 'historically sound' and much better than a 'Constitution' which, by royal pronouncement, supposedly was something lifeless, a mere piece of paper.

"It all made you feel that the court and the persons

close to the court had overslept by at least half a century. The restitution and extension of the 'estates'—that was to be the basis of it all. In the provincial capitals where until very recently some remnants of the feudal structure mentioned had survived, even if only as shadows of their former selves, the representatives of the nobility, the clergy, and of the municipal and rural corporations were to meet, and on certain occasions—this was to be an innovation—those chosen by the provincial diets were to meet in a great 'United Diet' ['*Vereinigter Landtag*'] in the state capital. Such a joint meeting of the provincial estates, so the thinking of men of influence went (that is, of men who by the king's wish and will possessed influence), was the limit of what one might offer the people. In such a solution, one would have the safeguard of tradition and, more important, the king's power and reputation would be preserved. Those were the notions to which Friedrich Wilhelm IV held very firmly.

"One might admit that there was some method in this approach, even a fair deal of honesty and good will, and if the whole affair had been staged 130 years earlier—although one might have had to omit the inconvenient figure of Friedrich Wilhelm I who would hardly have played his part in it—little might have been said against such joint labors of the 'estates' for at that time there was still some life in them, sickly and fenced-in though they were. There was no Prussian people yet. The whole country, in essence, consisted of our provinces East of the River Elbe, and these were agricultural provinces, where whatever subsisted aside from nobility, army, and civil service—about four million souls without a soul—did not count. But nothing remained of this patriarchal, absolutist state of affairs at the beginning of the last century when Friedrich Wilhelm IV ascended the throne.

"Everything had changed basically. Four million had

become twenty-four, and these twenty-four were no longer a miserable mob, a *misera plebs*, but free men, privately free at any rate, whom the world-changing ideas of the French Revolution had not passed by without a trace. The vast mistake of this clever and, in his fashion, honestly liberal-minded king was that he did not comprehend this historical change and that, in order to serve a preconceived opinion, he wished to put into practice *his* ideal, but not the ideals of his people. Friedrich Wilhelm IV acted as though he had been a professor who had set himself the task of judging between the *ethical* contents of an old feudal and a modern constitution and who had now found the greater ethical content to reside in the feudal one. But such findings were of no consequence. It is not the task of a government to express what is better or best. Rather it is the government's sole task to apply what the better and best parts of the nation wish to see expressed. It must concede such wishes, even if they contain errors.

"If a government is very strong—something it hardly ever is, however, where it resists the popular will—it can, for a longer or a shorter period, go its own way. But if resistance should continue, the government will almost always be defeated in the end. The weakness of Prussia's governments from the conclusion of the War of Liberation to the War of 1864 was their perpetual resistance to this simple maxim, whose undeniable truth one did not wish to comprehend. If Bismarck later enjoyed such phenomenal triumphs, it was, with all proper respect to his genius, due above all to the fact that he put his tremendous strength at the disposal of an idea that was alive in the soul of the German people.

"In this way, and in this way alone, was the German Empire built."[12]

The futility of reaction has seldom been described with

greater perception than by Fontane, the later *Kreuzzei-tung* correspondent, nor, one might add, with more transparent honesty. It is a quality which pervades his writing. As one reads both Fontane's private letters and his published works, one is struck by how little difference there is between the two in outlook and attitude. A political point might be made less sharply in a novel than in a letter to a close friend, but the point will be the same. There is—not only in regard to his political comments which after all take up but a relatively minor part of work—a happy absence of literary schizophrenia. Fontane the novelist, Fontane the poet, Fontane the travel writer, Fontane the historian, Fontane the theater critic, Fontane the private letter writer, all hold to the same opinions. His letters mirror his fiction, and his fiction his letters. For all their Prussian restraint, Fontane's pages too, in Goethe's phrase, appear as "fragments of a great confession."

But to return to 1848 and the reflections which were to follow it: Despite his shifting political sympathies, despite his growing skepticism about German Liberalism, Fontane would continue to see the revolution and its causes for what they were. Equally typical of his refusal ever to repudiate the essential truths of 1848 is a briefer passage from the *Wanderungen*. Describing the part played by a Mecklenburgian regiment in putting down violence in Dresden in 1848, he wrote, "Being definitely on the side of the latter [*i.e.*, on that of the soldiers] I may say all the more freely that nothing could be more foolish or unjust than to treat the crowds of the May revolution with contempt. The fault was that of the leaders. And here, too, distinctions should be made. Next to men driven by ambition or ill will were men motivated by genuine enthusiasm. The wish to create a republic is not necessarily stupid, and it certainly is not base."[13]

It was no longer Fontane's wish, however. He had come to appreciate the merits of a more established, traditional order:

> I, too, was born in Arcady
> I, too, was sworn to liberty . . .
> Down with the *possidentes beati*
> Was my wish, too—Oh *tempi passati*.[14]

"Freedom, of course," but mob rule was a bridge one passed over at one's own risk, after all. What in the end was better than any forty-eighter's ode against tyranny was "clear and firm laws; clear, firm commands."[15] *"Ordnung ist viel."*

"Work, and daily bread, and order," thinks Rienäcker in *Irrungen Wirrungen* as he watches a group of workers at lunch. "When our Brandenburgers marry, they don't talk of passion and love; they say '*Ich muss doch meine Ordnung haben*—I need things properly arranged.' And that is a good feature in the life of our people, and not even a prosaic one. For order is much, and there are times when it is everything."[16]

What added considerable strength to Fontane's Conservative outlook was his skepticism concerning the notion—so basic to nineteenth century Liberalism—of progress. "Tasks which are not capable of solution only serve to confuse mankind."[17] This skepticism, together with his reservations about the nature of man in the mass, ultimately was to prompt some pessimistic visions which remind one of both Jacob Burckhardt and Ortega y Gasset. "Technology and science aside," Fontane wrote to an English friend in the last year of his life, "I can see no universal progress." What he could see instead was the specter of war destruction. "If my glimpse into the future is correct, the thunderstorm will pass this time. The clouds are not heavy enough yet. The governments are still in charge, not the passions of the people. But once these play their part, we will have terrible struggles, and when they will be over, the world and the map will look different from today's."[18]

Fontane—and this makes him so superior a critic and so convincing where he does find fault—had come to have a great deal of confidence in the honesty, integrity, and ability of those who governed the country and rather little faith in an opposition which, whether Socialist or bourgeois, claimed to be speaking for the popular will. Others could be more merciless and more cutting than he in their political comments: one has only to think of Maximilian Harden or of the splendid cartoonists of the *Simplicissimus*. Oddly, the cumulative effect of their criticism is the weaker for it. They were always riding the attack; it seemed to be a matter of faith with them that a man who held public office was bound to be a fool and a knave. For all their talent, and for all their being right on more than one occasion, they sometimes remind one of the mythical Bavarian deputy's stubborn insistence, "Whatever the speaker before me may have said, I'm against it." The professional nay-sayer's lot is a doubtful one.[19]

Fontane, on the other hand, kept his sense of balance even after his appreciation of order had grown stronger than his urge to ring revolutionary tocsins. Second thoughts about 1848 he might have, but he would not turn into a dogmatic Tory or even into an enthusiastic National Liberal—he would not join that pro-Bismarck wing of the German Liberal movement which came closest, perhaps, among organized parties to representing his political convictions. "My political views—always, of course, somewhat shaky in nature—were usually identical with those of the National Liberals," he wrote in his late seventies only to retract the word "usually" almost as soon as it was written. A major reason for the retraction was his antagonism to the manner in which the National Liberals were conducting their political battles. He noted that, "in essence, the opinions of most educated Prussians are identical with the attitude that it expressed by the program of the National Liberals." Yet the party had failed to play a truly decisive part in the political life of Fontane's generation. The explanation, he thought, was in the melody rather than in the words; it seemed to him a matter not of ideas but of "the *tone* in which the principles were being advocated. The Progressives are self-righteous and dogmatic too, but it is the dogma of a rabid sectarian rather than that of a spiritually and morally arrogant know-it-all. And arrogance hurts more feelings than rabidness. Politicians might smile at these sentences, but there may be others who will see what is correct about them."[20]

Hence, when it came to voting, neither National Liberals nor Conservatives had his very certain support. "I am leaving now," he wrote to his publisher's son on the day of a Reichstag election in 1890, "to put my ballot into a box for the first time in many, many years; which one? In my embarrassment, I arrived at a decision by counting buttons. Only he who knows nothing knows it definitely."[21]

A position he was equally unwilling to assume, no matter how much sense the soldiers' side of 1848 came to make to him, was that of the patriotic flag-waver. *Hurrahpatriotismus* remained anathema to him. The Prussian historical ballads he wrote in his youth had been notably free of Teutonic heroics, Gallic villainies, and similar postures.[22] A later suggestion that he write some more patriotic poetry on order—his earlier poems had been spontaneous as well as restrained—repelled him. "You can't imagine how I hate such rhymes."[23] His patriotism was that of a man who had very much kept his reason. "The book," he told his publisher about *Vor dem Sturm*, "is the expression of a definite view of the world and of life. It defends religion, morality, fatherland; but it is full of hatred against 'the blue corn flower'[24] and 'With God for King and Fatherland!' In other words, it is against the phraseology and caricature of these three."[25]

Fontane knew the realities of Prussia's past and present too well to accept the pomposities of Emperor's Birthday oratory or to rewrite history in the manner of *Turnvater* Jahn or Heinrich von Treitschke or the pan-Germans. Describing the long struggle between Wends and Germans in Brandenburg, for example, he wrote: "In glorious naïveté do the [German] chroniclers tell us about the endless perfidies of the Germans. The explanation is that, imbued with party spirit and blinded in the service of a great idea, they always assumed their own perfidies to be justified. Wend treason, however, was treason pure and simple—exposed without glory, in ordinary, naked ugliness. The Wend simply was a 'dog,' without honor and without rights, and if he should unexpectedly get up and bite his adversary that made him faithless."[26]

Or, even closer to his century and political convictions, there are the reflections of Dubslav von Stechlin which might be Fontane's own: "*Ja, der alte Fritz!*—Oh yes, Frederick the Great! One can't think highly enough of him, but in one respect I believe we see him in the wrong light—we aristocrats in particular. He was not for us as much as we always believe or at least profess to believe for external consumption. He was for himself and for the country or, as he liked to say, 'for the state.'

"What was the real situation? We had the honor of being allowed to go hungry and thirsty and to die for king and fatherland, but we were never asked whether

it suited us to do so. Yes, now and then we were told
that we were 'noblemen' and hence had more 'honor.' But
that was it. In his inmost soul, the words were those he
yelled to the grenadiers at Torgau.[27] We were raw material, and he usually looked at us with very critical eyes.
All in all, dear Count, I find our year 1813 very much
greater, because there was less of the character of commands, and more freedom and voluntary decision in
everything that happened then. I am not in favor of the
patented freedom of the Party Liberals, but I am in favor
of a certain degree of freedom in general. And unless all
the signs deceive me, our people, too, slowly realize that—
in a very practical and egotistical way if nothing else—
we shall fare best if we have that."[28]

Fontane's choice of Dubslav von Stechlin, good Prussian squire and true, as spokesman for his own convictions
may suggest one final reason for his kind of Conservatism.
During his years with the *Kreuzzeitung,* and while col-
lecting his material for the *Wanderungen,* Fontane had
come into contact with a fair number of country squires,
and he had found that, by and large, they were people
much after his own heart—by and large, for Fontane
would not have been Fontane if here, too, he had not
seen the flaws as well as the charm and had not been
curious and perceptive enough to hold both sides of the
Order of the Black Eagle up to his eyes.

CHAPTER III

The Two Faces of the Prussian Squire

... Thus blessings still flow from the hand
Of von Ribbeck on Ribbeck in Havelland.
THEODOR FONTANE, *"Herr von Ribbeck,"* 1889

I am moving farther and farther away from my beloved
nobility. ... They should all be boiled alive.
THEODOR FONTANE to Georg Friedlaender,
April 12, 1894

IN CONTEMPORARY AMERICAN DEMONOLOGY, the Prussian *Junker* seems to occupy a position somewhere between ogre and werewolf. "The Junkers, who were to play such a vital role in modern Germany," William Shirer has written in his vastly popular *The Rise and Fall of the Third Reich,* were "a unique product of Prussia. They were, as they said, a master race. It was they who occupied the land conquered from the Slavs and who farmed it on large estates farmed by these Slavs, who became landless serfs quite different from those in the West. ... The Prussian Junker was not a man of leisure. He worked hard at managing his large estate, much as a factory manager does today. His landless laborers were treated as virtual slaves. On his large properties he was the absolute lord. There were no large towns nor any substantial middle class, as there were in the West, whose civilizing influence might rub against him. In contrast to the cultivated *grand seigneur* in the West, the Junker developed into a rude, domineering, arrogant type of man, without cultivation or culture, aggressive, conceited, ruthless, narrow-minded and given to a petty profit-seeking that some German historians noted in the private life of Otto von Bismarck, the most successful of the Junkers."[1]

Professor Louis L. Snyder, in a chapter of his *German Nationalism, The Tragedy of a People* entitled "Militarism; The Development of War-Cult Extremism from Karl von Clausewitz to Ewald Banse," has traced Prussian militarism and *Junker* arrogance back equally far. "The rise of Prussia took place in an atmosphere of violence and blood-letting. . . . Brandenburg, an area of savagery and conquest, was dominated by a ruthless, arrogant, ignorant nobility, many of whom were of Slavic origin. The Hohenzollern dynasty, whose original home was in Swabia in southwestern Germany, appropriated the Teutonic order in Brandenburg at the end of the fifteenth century. Out of the union of the Hohenzollern dynasty and the wild, unprincipled Junkers of Brandenburg came Brandenburg-Prussia and eventually Prussia."[2]

A. J. P. Taylor, after an indictment which bears some startling similarities to that of William Shirer, has granted the *Junkers*, for all their vices, some considerable managerial ability, but even that compliment is given in anger: "The Prussian Junkers, one might say, were politically in the Stone Age; economically and administratively they looked forward to the age of steel and electricity. They were barbarians who had learned to handle a rifle and, still more, bookkeeping by double entry."[3]

Not all that has been said about the *Junker* is quite that graphic or contemptuous. Among American historians, for instance, both Gordon Craig and Koppel S. Pinson have notably departed from the clichés about the *Junker* which seem to be passed on from writer to writer with the respect and care one might more reasonably expect from fundamentalist Bible criticism.[4] Still, as far as the prevailing mood is concerned, it is passages such as those from Shirer, Snyder, and Taylor which tend to set the tone. There certainly is no shortage of quotations similar to theirs. Fontane's views, on the other hand, were somewhat more complex.

Not that he was insensitive to the Prussian squire's

many failings—he would be bitter and outspoken about those—but he was equally able to appreciate his many virtues. Here as elsewhere Fontane was aided by his ability to see the essence as well as the appearance. There is a wonderfully symbolic scene in the opening pages of the *Wanderungen* describing Fontane's encounter, on the Zieten estate at Wustrau, with the portraits of sixteen officers from Hans Joachim von Zieten's regiment, all painted between 1749 and 1751, and all of them unspeakably martial in appearance. "Some of them looked as though they had been painted in blood." The visitor's first impulse was to depart in some haste, but if he managed to stay for only a few minutes, he might see the canvases in another light. "The old waxed mustachios begin to assume human shape, and in the end you will recognize the well-known Brandenburgian and Pomeranian faces behind all this apparatus of horror and see that the martial expressions were exaggerated into all but diabolical ones merely as part of *being on duty*."[5]

Whether that is the full explanation or not, the squires of his own period who appear in Fontane's books and letters are painted in champagne as much as in blood. Looks and manners of the Prussian aristocracy had mellowed in the generations since Zieten's. Effi's father, Ritterschaftsrat von Briest, is a "well-preserved gentleman in his fifties, of decidedly good nature."[6] Baron Osten in *Irrungen Wirrungen* is a "charming old gentleman and jolly fellow, although something of a fox, too." "Like all Brandenburgers," someone notes.[7]

Like many of them, certainly, Osten is fond of the good things of life: of comfortable hotels and very fresh lobsters and properly chilled white wines. One lives well in Fontane's novels and world. The linen is heavy, the furniture is kept polished, and the drinks offered are Veuve Cliquot and Courvoisier, not mead.

Nor is it a matter of surface manners alone—if there be such a thing as "surface manners alone." The squires in Fontane's novels may not be mental giants—they will often prefer horses to books—but they are honest and decent people and by no means fools. They can also be very kind. No one has erected a more touching poetic memorial to the kindly country squire than Fontane in his *"Herr von Ribbeck auf Ribbeck im Havelland,"* the *Junker* who never lets a harvest season pass without stuffing his pockets with pears and distributing them to the children of the neighborhood, a practice which he continues even in death, for he has had a pear tree planted on his grave:

> And when a boy walks by the grave
> The tree will whisper: "Come have a pear."
> And when a girl goes strolling by
> It's, "Come pick a fruit, my lassie there."
> Thus blessings still flow from the hand
> Of von Ribbeck on Ribbeck in Havelland.[8]

Kindly or not, almost all of his squires are men of courage. The word "duty" has a special and inescapable meaning to them. To write a history of the von Rohr family, Fontane noted, was to write a history of Brandenburg-Prussia and of its bloodiest battles—"a Rohr was always there:"

> *Bei Leuthen, Lipa, Leipzig,*
> *An der Katzbach und an der Schlei*
> *Von Fehrbellin bis Sedan—*
> *Ein Rohr war immer dabei.*[9]

At the same time, heroic poses had better be avoided. "'What matters for a Brandenburger is to have been there,'" is one of Major (Retired) von Stechlin's frequent sayings. "'Everything else is in God's hands.' And he smiled whenever he said this, which left his listeners in doubt each time whether he was speaking seriously or in jest."[10] Quite possibly the latter, for the Major also observes that "heroism is an exceptional state of affairs, and the product, in most cases, of the lack of any alternative."[11]

Simplicity, sobriety, and the absence of pose mark the squires' outlook quite generally. *Esse quam videri* might be the motto of many of them. Dubslav von Stechlin, proud as he is of his estate, persistently calls Castle Stechlin "*Haus Stechlin*" on his stationery.[12] Occasionally, the *Junker's* lack of pretense may indicate nothing more complex than a certain lack of imagination—"Briest was a man one could live with, although he was a bit prosaic"[13]— but it is not attributable to any lack of pride, particularly family pride. Stechlin has the quiet confidence of those "who had been there since before the arrival of the Hohenzollerns."[14] He also is plagued by constant money worries which might have proved fatal but for two people: "his old friend Baruch Hirschfeld," owner of the clothing store in the neighboring town, and Dubslav's sister Adelheid, "prioress at Convent Wutz." The prioress, while disapproving of her brother's style of life, would help out when necessary out of "a general Stechlin loyalty. Prussia was something, and so was Brandenburg. But what mattered the most were the Stechlins, and she found the thought of having the castle pass into different hands unbearable. . . ."[15]

Pride, at the same time, ought not to be allowed to turn into arrogance. If Stechlin speaks about his family tree's venerable age at all, it is with a healthy portion of irony. Fontane's squire is no snob. Von Rienäcker, the protagonist of *Irrungen Wirrungen*, has the "attractive and refreshing tendency of all Brandenburgian aristocrats to enjoy talking to ordinary people—*Leuten aus dem*

Volke—to prefer it to talking to 'the educated classes.' "[16] At times, this common touch, together with his social conscience, leads the squire rather far afield from the prejudices of the usual *Kreuzzeitung* editorial. "Every real *Junker*," someone comments in *Der Stechlin*, "has a bit of the Social Democrat in his bones."[17]

Nor are the wholly eccentric missing from Fontane's gallery of squires. The most appealing among them may be the eighteenth century squire Georg Moritz von Rohr. Outliving four wives, his private funeral oration each time was, "If God taketh away, I can take another," whereupon he proceeded to court his next bride. Getting odder with advancing age, he climbed a poplar tree on his estate to hold his personal devotions. His white hair blowing in the breeze, he would sing his hymns in a loud, clear voice, "grotesque and touching at the same time. For the village youth, the former predominated, however, and a few exuberant souls partly loosened the branch by means of a saw, and when the next day he meant to take his place in the tree, he crashed to the ground together with the branch. There is no report of his being angry. . . . "[18]

But the squire in the tree is the exception. Usually, one stays on the ground and observes the proprieties, at the risk of hurting oneself far more than the hymn-singing von Rohr. Baron Innstetten will knowingly ruin his life by fighting a duel in whose validity he at bottom no longer believes. Honor matters. Conventions may be doubted, but they must be respected. "One is not just an individual, living in isolation; one is part of a group, and we must forever show our consideration for that group. If I could live in isolation, I would let things be. . . ." This is the argument which in the end decides Innstetten that he must fight his duel.[19] On a less tragic plane, there is Baron Osten auf Wietzendorf, who, perhaps to be on the safe side, in his own words, is so "conservative even in small things" that he stays at the same hotel on all his trips to Berlin.[20]

Thus far, Fontane's analysis of Prussian aristocractic qualities may have contained few surprises except, possibly, to believers in some sort of Prusso-German original sin. Courtliness, charm, kindness, courage, loyalty, family pride—are not these the values of any aristocracy, whether in Devonshire, Normandy, Virginia, or Brandenburg? One virtue that may not have been anticipated, however, particularly since the diagnosis that National Socialism was a Prussian disease still finds its supporters, is the squire's air of tolerance. The quality, alas, is of a special sort: it is not for export beyond the manor. The squire's public political behavior is likely to be selfish and archaic:

> From Köckeritz and Lüderitz
> From Krachten and from Itzenplitz
> Preserve us, God, we beg you.[21]

But manage to visit a von Itzenplitz or a von Köckeritz at home, and you will find him tolerant, broad-minded, and Liberal: "Overnight, he has become a different man. As soon as he is no longer on the defensive, and no longer besieged in Kreistag or Reichstag (where, following old tactics to the letter, he feels that the best defense lies in the attack), he takes off the spiked coat of mail which he himself has found uncomfortable by now and puts on the imaginary garment of his ancient virtues. These virtues are a good deal of kindness, an even greater one of common sense, and the greatest of all: a critical spirit. With a pleasure that soon infects his audience, he will put everything under the magnifying glass of his skepticism, uttering opinions that are so radical and progressive that one would think the river flowing by his old craggy tower was named the Hudson or the Potomac, and not the

Nieplitz or the Notte. What is behind it is nothing but *jeu d'esprit*, however, and there is not the least intention of remembering any of it in the sobering hours of the following morning, let alone of doing anything about it. Even as a pure game it is remarkable, and it proves sufficiently that there is something bright and sharp and sophisticated in him and that the roots of that selfishness which one so strongly dislikes in him might have many reasons—but that narrow-mindedness is not among them. The way he views things, on the contrary, is sharp and penetrating. . . . The reason he fights so hard and bitterly for his existence is not that he cannot see where his adversaries are right, but rather because he *can* see just that. What he cannot do is to take the final step leading from recognition to admission.

"All in all, they are better than their reputation, these much-maligned '*Junkers*'—different and better. . . ."²²

In his fiction, where Itzenplitz and Köckeritz have been given names such as Stechlin and Osten, Fontane reiterates the same theme. At a luncheon with some young lieutenants, old Baron Osten concludes an angry tirade against Bismarck by saying: "I can't stand this cult. . . . But the gentlemen are silent. Do speak, please. Believe me, I can hear other opinions. I can stand them; I am not the way he is. Do speak, Herr von Wedell, do speak."²³ Dubslav von Stechlin, whose political sympathies are somewhere to the right of Prince Metternich's but whose *Hausatmosphäre* is Liberal,²⁴ feels as Osten does. "He liked to hear an opinion freely uttered, the more drastic and the more extreme the better. It was far from his mind that the opinion should resemble his own. Almost the contrary. Paradoxes were his passion. "'I am not clever enough to make them myself, but I am happy when others do; there is always something to them. Unassailable truths don't exist, or if they do, they are dull.' "25

As Fontane grew older, his attitude toward Osten and his friends underwent something of a shift. Like a good Chinese cook, Fontane still mixed the sweet with the sour when presenting the Prussian squire to his reader, but the sour came to predominate. Personal experience as well as general observations may account for the changed proportions. Though he took pains to distinguish between the *Kreuzzeitung's* relentless public anti-Liberalism on the one hand, and the rather more easy-going private views of its editors on the other, he had long had his reservations about the paper's editorial policies. Conservative Fontane might be by temperament and conviction, but the *Kreuzzeitung's* narrow-minded, uncompromising brand of "With God for King and Fatherland" was hardly to his taste. What in the end brought the issue to a head, and made him part company with the paper—and to some extent with what it stood for— were some very personal worries about his future.26 The *Kreuzzeitung* had always treated him shabbily, he felt, and at the age of fifty he became sufficiently concerned over the paper's lack of any retirement plan, and hence over his own financial insecurity, to quit his employment. The letter in which he told his wife of the decision contained some caustic words about the business practices of the Prussian *Junker's* favorite newspaper which went beyond the immediate issue: "It is *indecent* to be using big phrases all the time, to quote scripture and Christianity all the time and never to exercise a *necessary* consideration which is being shown (often and generously so) by Jews and industrialists and all those who are always being attacked in our God-fearing columns."27

He did not cease to admire the squire's more attractive

qualities,[28] but he found the discrepancy between the Prussian aristocracy's private and public selves increasingly distasteful. Nor may the astonishing lack of appreciation shown to his literary work by the Prussian aristocracy have been entirely without influence on his shifting views. Much of that work—his early poems, the *Wanderungen,* many of his novels—had been a literary monument to the Prussian squire; yet the people who understood and praised Fontane more often than not belonged to the proper (and frequently Jewish) bourgeois society of Berlin rather than to the proper regiments of Potsdam. Fontane's poem, *"An meinem Fünfundsiebzigsten,"* with its famous last line, *"Kommen Sie, Cohn"* (were not the Cohns, after all, of a nobility older than the von Itzenplitz?), may be the most obvious expression of his disappointment over having attracted only a part of the audience at which he had aimed. One should be cautious, however, about attributing too much importance to hurt vanity. Fontane was not the man to transform personal slights into sweeping world views. Besides, there was nothing imaginary about the squire's failings which came to distress him so much.

To strike the proper balance, he wrote his publisher, "between respect for our country squire in a human and social sense, and doubts about him in a political sense, is a dance on eggs which I do not care to perform every day."[29] The doubts more and more revolved around three things: the squire's arrogance, his political backwardness, and with that backwardness his worst sin: his vast selfishness.

Not all of Major von Stechlin's and Councilor von Briest's historic counterparts, Fontane knew, were as unpretentious in their ways. There was Ludwig von der Marwitz, for example, early nineteenth century Conservative and opponent of reform, who described a meeting with Goethe in the following sentence, cited by Fontane: "He [Goethe] was a tall and handsome man, always in embroidered court dress, who showed you that he was a minister and well represented the dignity of his office, although the natural and free decorum of the aristocrat was lacking." In his polite fashion, Fontane was appalled by the arrogance betrayed by Marwitz. Goethe, he wrote, "was a respectful minister and a great poet, the friend of his prince and the shining star of his court, but having been born the son of a citizen of Frankfurt, he 'lacked the natural and free decorum of the aristocrat.' Some indefinable something was missing—perhaps the great school of the Regiment Gendarmes."[30]

Even worse than the occasional lapse into arrogance, a fault which it seemed to Fontane was in danger of increasing amid the prosperous atmosphere of the new Reich[31] was the squire's general selfishness. "Our nobles, I know I may speak to *you* like that," wrote Fontane to his old and aristocratic friend Mathilde von Rohr, "in most cases are noble only because of the 'von' in front of their names. They insist on their privileges, but attempt to evade their duties."[32] Their political organization, the Conservative Party, seemed based on prejudice and on self-interest pure and simple, and not on any set of principles. The Prussian aristocracy's characteristic political posture was one of "pseudo-Conservatism, which in the final analysis wants nothing but its own interests and whatever might serve them."[33]

It was not Fontane's kind of Conservatism, nor did it fit his (or old von Briest's or von Stechlin's) definition of the aristocratic. "And my father," Effi Briest reminisces in the presence of her somewhat eccentric friend, the pharmacist Gieshübler in Kessin, "it must have been more than a hundred times that he told me: 'Effi, *here* it is and here only, and when Froben changed horses, he was a noble,[34] and when Luther said "here I stand," he even more certainly was a noble.' "[35] "By the way," wrote Fontane to his wife, let me say very emphatically that what I call 'noble' is not reserved to the class called 'nobility'; it is something that you will find in all classes. It is a feeling for the commonweal, for the ideal, and a dislike of the most narrow."[36]

The Prussian nobility he watched in Bismarck's Reich displayed far too few of these virtues, and in his last years, Fontane came to feel that as a class it had outlived its usefulness. Its claim to be able and entitled to rule the country, he said, was "naive."[37] The Prussian country squire "has become unpalatable."[38] "I am moving farther and farther away from my beloved nobility. . . . They should all be boiled alive. They are outdated."[39]

In words less violent, some of his novels reiterate the same theme. Implied in *Irrungen Wirrungen* is a mood of resignation, a feeling that the aristocracy has become devitalized to the point of being incapable of coping with its times. The novel's plot is simple enough: it revolves around a love affair between a seamstress, Lene, and an aristocratic officer, Botho von Rienäcker. The affair comes to an end when Botho, in order to rescue his family's finances, marries the lightheaded daughter of a wealthy country squire. Lene, honest and solid and good, and in love with Botho as he is with her, is the girl he should have married instead, and he knows it. Were the class barriers between them really that high? Were family pressures that strong? Yes and no; at any rate, Botho does not have the strength to overcome them, or even to try. He and Lene accept this weakness without rebellion, just as both resign themselves to the lesser happiness which their respective marriages will offer them. It is a typical Fontane theme: one always settles for less than the dream in his novels. No man is truly free, hence let him make his peace with fate, with society, with whatever the forces that limit his freedom. *Das grosse Glück* forever is elusive. But Botho von Rienäcker, officer and Prussian squire, seems more thoroughly defeated by society than many another figure in Fontane. He is, in truth, as weak as any hero in a play by Arthur Schnitzler.

The book's closing scene sums up the mood. Lene has finally been persuaded to marry a man closer to her station in life, a decent and kindly sectarian by the name of Gideon Franke. Baroness Rienäcker, entirely unaware of her husband's past association with Lene, reads the wedding announcement in the morning paper and is much amused by Franke's first name. Rienäcker's reply, which ends the book, is "*Was hast du nur gegen Gideon, Käthe? Gideon ist besser als Botho.*"

It is a scene, once again, which Schnitzler might have written. The atmosphere no longer is that of Potsdam but of *fin de siècle* Vienna. "And nothing can be done about it. . . ." A weary Habsburg, not a vehement Hohenzollern, might be Emperor in Berlin.

The same theme of a nobility which for all its virtues has outlived its day is treated even more plainly and with sharper emphasis on its political implications in *Der Stechlin*. "I love our old families," says Pastor Lorenzen. "I have cause to love them, and I just about believe that everybody loves them. The old families are still popular, even today. But they waste these sympathies, they throw them away, when after all everybody is in need of such sympathies, every person and every class. Our old families all suffer from the deception 'that things could not run without them—*dass es ohne sie nicht gehe.*' But that is far from being so. Things could assuredly run without them. They no longer are the pillar on which everything rests. They are the old roof, made of stone and covered with moss, which still bears and presses down but which no longer protects us from rain and hail. Who can tell, the days of an aristocracy may return. For the time being, however, we see democracy wherever we look. A new era is beginning. I believe a better one and a happier one. And if not happier, at least an age with more oxygen in the air, an age where we can breathe better. And the more freely a man breathes, the better he lives."[40]

Fontane's sentiments revive memories of an earlier indictment of the nobility, delivered, again in sorrow as much as in anger, by one of the greatest of German late Romantic poets, Baron Joseph von Eichendorff. Both Eichendorff and Fontane were essentially Conservative, both were men of letters and poets rather than political commentators, yet both were sharp observers of the contemporary aristocracy, and both found it wanting, mainly for its selfishness and its inability to find its proper place in the modern world. "Very old people," wrote Eichendorff, "feel that they can still remember the good old days rather well. Yet in reality, these days were neither good nor old; they were a caricature of what was good and old. The saber had become a dress sword, the helmet a pointed wig, the lord of the castle a retired colonel of Hussars, besieged and surrounded ever more closely on his dull country estate . . . by industrialists. In a word, it was the age of chivalry grown tired and brittle, using powder to disguise the considerable mould in its hair, comparable to a smug old dandy who still prances around the fair ladies and who cannot understand it and will become very touchy if the world no longer thinks him young." The aristocracy had squandered its true mission: "The chivalrous protection of all that is great and noble and beautiful—no matter how and where it is found among people—and the mediation between the ever-changing new and the ever-lasting old," and Eichendorff could see no signs that the aristocracy would ever recover that mission again.[41]

Nor could Fontane, even if, like Pastor Lorenzen, he to the end remained fond of the Prussian squires whose defects he had come to see so distinctly. Fontane's views, let it be reiterated, show less of a change over the years than a summary of them might seem to indicate. The young Fontane never saw all squires as jolly Ribbecks, presenting pears to village youths. The older Fontane did not constantly wish to boil all *Junkers* alive. Most of us, after all, are capable of loving and hating the same person or the same object at rapidly alternating moments. So was Fontane. For all their "enormous faults," the squires of Brandenburg remained close to his heart; they were his kind of people.[42] His *Junker* bears little resemblance to the monster that too many writers have made of him—not in his private self, that is, where he remains charming, open-minded, civilized, and very human. In his public self—with his political myopia, his selfishness, his *Kreuzzeitung* Conservatism—he comes closer to reminding one of his caricature in *Simplicissimus* or *Punch*, although the militancy and the bluster may be hiding nothing more evil than his discomfort at being incapable of changing with the times. (One thinks of the character in Max Frisch's *Stiller* who is "understandably opposed to the future.") The desire for world conquest is not among the squire's sins; egotism is. Still, the melancholy charge remains that the political life of the new Reich was badly served by Prussia's old aristocracy. The charge is all the more convincing and disturbing since it did not please Fontane to make it.

CHAPTER IV

Workers, Vicars, Bankers

> A new power has established itself: the intelligent bourgeoisie, its face turned away from the medieval, and toward progress. Free from tradition and prejudice, it lives for the sake of *this* world and sees happiness in property and in the celebration of the secular.
>
> Will it succeed? Some say yes, some doubt it. But no matter what the answer will be, we should first of all rejoice in the natural growth of all that lives, unencumbered by the thought of whether this development represents a step upwards into higher regions or downwards into death and destruction. That which grows, be it good or bad, takes the place of that which falls, and before long it will fall in turn. That is the eternal law.
>
> THEODOR FONTANE, *Wanderungen durch die Mark Brandenburg*

FONTANE'S VIEWS of other groups and classes in Wilhelmian Germany resemble that of the nobility in sharpness of vision, and, since he was as dubious as Major von Stechlin about "undeniable truths," in lack of dogma. He had few sympathies for the Social Democrats, yet his eyes were open to the social realities of his day. The Socialists, he thought, were people who wished to "turn the world upside down" for reasons that did not convince him at all, and the Marxist program struck him as little better than an attempt to justify theft.[1] At the same time, the working class figures of his novels, as in *Irrungen Wirrungen,* are drawn with profound sympathy, and he was aware of the forces which made the period a potentially revolutionary one.[2] If he never learned to love the Social Democrats, he nevertheless could see that their kind of opposition provided an utterly necessary stimulus in German life. "If the Social Democrats did not exist, . . . the situation would be hopeless for the foreseeable future; as things are, change

39

is at least possible, though for the worse, too, of course."[3]

Besides, his admiration for the capitalist was small, particularly if the latter was of the newly rich variety. In part, his dislike of the bourgeoisie was quite unpolitical. What exasperated him most, perhaps, was what has made many an artist before and since turn his back on the bourgeois. "I hate the bourgeois spirit," he wrote, "as though I were a sworn Social Democrat. 'He is a fool, but his father owns that big building'—that is a form of admiration with which I have no longer any patience."[4] "They all pretend to have ideals, they talk forever of 'the good, the beautiful, and the true,' and in reality they genuflect only before the golden calf."[5] Or there is the memorable description of *l'après-midi d'un bourgeois*, with its echoes of Madame de Staël's sighs, brought on by her German travels, of the apparent compulsion on the part of her hosts "to offer every food, every wine, with a solicitude and an insistance which the foreigner will find mortally tedious."[6] Not the foreigner only, for here, as seen by Fontane, was the all too comfortable *Bürger* of his period, "with his pettiness and his endless desire to be admired for nothing. Father bourgeois has had his portrait painted, and asks that I declare this daub to be a Velasquez. Mother bourgeois has bought herself a lace stole and treats that purchase as An Event. Everything bought or 'offered' is accompanied by a glance saying, 'Happy person who is allowed to eat of *this* cake and to drink of this wine.' . . . A dinner of roast goose and Zeltinger and meringues at which the hostess is all smiles and imagines that she has taken me out of the humdrum of my daily existence for two hours is cheap in itself and made doubly cheap by the attitude which accompanies it."[7]

He also had his doubts about the political acumen of the goose-eating bourgeoisie. The squire's days were over, but Fontane felt by no means certain that the new class had the intelligence and ability to act as his political heir. However, once again, heartfelt though his contempt for the vulgarities of the *nouveau riche,* profound though his doubts whether the German businessman and banker could ever play the political role of his French or English equivalent, there was no blanket condemnation of "the bourgeoisie." He could also see its more established segment, "intelligent . . . its face turned . . . toward progress; free from tradition and prejudice."[8] Besides, amusingly and sensibly enough, he had always excepted the *very* rich from his strictures. Big businessmen "who employ 5,000 people, found new manufacturing cities, send out expeditions to colonize Africa" and the like could be fascinating people:[9]

> My interest in money and such like stuff
> Only begins with Prince Demidov
> With Yusupov and Dolgorucky
> With slave-holders from South Kentucky
> With Mackay, and Gould, and Bennet, and Astors
> *Our* atmosphere's that of threadbare pastors.[10]

If the bourgeoisie's two faces—progressive in parliament, unbearable at home—were the reverse of the nobility's, another group again reminds us of the squire's public conservatism and private charm. The group is that of the "threadbare pastors," or rather of the Prussian clergy in general.

"And now my favorites of them all, my country pastors and Vicars of Wakefield! I know the sun of popular favor does not smile upon you. And, indeed, if one sees you in solemn procession toward the synod, wearing tailcoats and that look which seems to be another of the special contributions of our North German Protestantism, and if one hears you talk about the spirit of the age, which you would like to change but cannot change, and about the

Jews, who should be converted but who in the end would rather not—if one sees all this one might once more pray 'May God preserve us.' "[11]

But one would be wrong, for in his own element, among his roses and in his vicarage, the country pastor becomes perceptive and kind:

"Here, too, I observed that the very opposite of the public image . . . was correct. Having said before that I never observed the narrow-mindedness of which the country squire stands accused, I should add that I never found any truth in the accusation of intolerance against the country parson. There may have been, and there may still be, individual cases of intolerance, but I have not seen any. I have never heard the rationalists judge the Orthodox, or the Orthodox the rationalists, with any real malice, not even in times of the most burning arguments and of open battle. Instead, one detected good will toward the adversary even in the very questions that made him an adversary. A general mood of good will— based on a true understanding of a profession and a vocation aimed at conciliation and love—showed itself in all things, great and small, and revived in me the romantic enthusiasm of my youth for the country pastor."[12] Once again, one may feel transported from the River Nieplitz to the River Thames: in his treatment of the clergy, as in many other of his attitudes, Fontane brings to mind his contemporary and startlingly close English literary counterpart, Anthony Trollope.

Complex and varied as Fontane's views of Prusso-German society then were, several common denominators do stand out. One, of course, is his consistent preference for observable fact over inherited opinion. Another is the absence of the rebel's pose. He accepted the world for what it was, and by and large he liked it; ". . . honor," he wrote to a friend, "admire, and *still* have an opinion of your own and the courage of an occasional 'No.'" There, he felt, lay "that freedom for which I have been sighing for forty years now."[13] The third and last common denominator is his tolerance, a tolerance of the most impressive variety, since it was not based (as one suspects it sometimes is in our age) on *ennui* or the absence of strong convictions. Having described the vulgarity and parochialism—"*sächsische Spiessbürger*"—of Karlsbad's tourist society with considerable annoyance, he added that on the other hand, "I agree with Bismarck. *'Es muss auch Lippen geben*—there must be room for citizens of Lippe too.' And if 'Lippese,' then certainly Slovenes, Rumanians, Serbians. They may not provide virtue, but they provide life. . . ."[14]

The same spirit animates his opinions on the specific issues and events of his day. His enthusiasm for the Franco-Prussian War was muted at best.[15] When it was over, and Alsace-Lorraine had been annexed, he warned that whether one liked it or not, the people of those provinces were French rather than German in loyalty and sentiment. Having visited the region as a war correspondent, he expressed his doubts whether the German officers and administrators who had arrived with the occupation government had the temper or the ability for their posts.[16] Zabern and many years of German blunders in Alsace-Lorraine seem to be anticipated in the conversation between two German occupation officials, both Uhlan officers, overheard by Fontane in the train to Strasbourg and recorded by him with little pleasure: "Thus, the two gentlemen talked of their deeds, agreed that one was dealing with a 'gang,' that one could wrap them around one's fingers 'if one knew how to deal with them,' and that 'stern measures' were therefore indicated."[17]

All the same, he had no objections to defense spending, unpleasant Uhlans or no. "I do not understand the Pro-

gressives," he wrote his son about the army budget of
1886. "I am confident that the people who direct our
government do not wish to make Germany an armed
camp because they enjoy doing so. They do what they
must." What mattered, he thought, was that "I can drink
my coffee tomorrow without a Frenchman in it (and he
without me)."[18]

He wished to be equally free of domestic threats to
his liberty, and to fair play. He disliked Bismarck's anti-
Catholic campaign.[19] He reacted to the antisubversion bill
of 1894, the so-called *Umsturzvorlage*, with even stronger
misgivings. The bill would have provided for prison terms
of up to two years for offenses as vaguely defined as
"enticing various classes of the population to commit acts
of violence against one another," or "publicly attacking,
in a manner insulting or designed to endanger the public
peace, religion, monarchy, marriage, family, or property."[20]
The bill so bothered Fontane that he took the unusual
step of adding his name to a public protest against it and
agreed to solicit the signatures of some socially prominent
friends of his as well: "The names must say: 'we, too, the
most loyal, feel threatened. No one is safe.' "[21] "Usually,
I am not in favor of demonstrations and protests. I know
that nothing is ever eaten as hot as it comes out of the
oven. Still, the mere idea of presenting the famous nation
of 'poets and philosophers' . . . with such nonsense is
monstrous, and a disgrace before Europe. . . ."[22] (The
sentiments, it turned out, would be shared by a majority
of Reichstag deputies, who in a vote taken on May 11,
1895, decisively defeated the antisubversion bill.[23])

He opposed censorship of the arts, no matter what the
excuse. Foreign artists had sent some interesting works,
he wrote of the Great Berlin Art Exhibit of 1895. "Most
of what *we* have exhibited, as usual, is dull. We won't
have complete art until we have complete freedom, and

I don't care if there'll be some obscenities and some impertinences. They won't last three days. Those in charge believe, in every field, that they can preserve what is dead by pickling it. That is a bit of stupidity which I find incomprehensible, considering the intelligence of the upper strata of our society."[24]

These and other opinions may well be more distinguished for their acumen than for their originality, reflecting as they do the outlook of many an enlightened and intelligent German Conservative or many a pragmatic and intelligent German Liberal of the time. On three larger topics, however, Fontane's views deserve a more detailed analysis for their contemporary insights as well as for some of the prophetic judgments they contain. These topics are Bismarck, the role of Prussia, and what Fontane held to be the intrinsic structural defects of the Reich Bismarck had built.

CHAPTER V

The Two Faces of Otto von Bismarck

> There is a Mecklenburg story in which a Berliner, who
> has gone swimming in Warnemünde, wants to know
> "what a pilot is" and asks a native. The reply is: "a
> pilot is a pilot; and what a pilot is, everybody knows."
> It is much the same with Bismarck. He has founded
> the German Empire. As soon as one tries to say more
> one flounders.
>
> THEODOR FONTANE to Gustav Keyssner, April 2, 1896

THE ONE CONSTANT in Fontane's attitude toward Bismarck
was the fascination which the person of the Chancellor
held for him. "When he sneezes, or says 'Bless you!'"
Fontane wrote to his daughter, "I find that more interesting than the forensic wisdom of six Progressives."[1] Life
had been drained of most of its excitements for him, he
wrote as he turned seventy:

> Truth to tell, I no longer care.
> Some men grow rich, some waste their property.
> But Bismarck now: What will yet happen there?
> Now *that* is something I'd still like to see.[2]

In almost everything he had written in the preceding
quarter century, he told Maximilian Harden in 1894,
"there is the specter of *der Schwefelgelbe*.[3] Even if the
conversation should just barely touch on him, he is always there. . . ."[4]

At times, fascination equaled admiration. As a public
speaker, thought Fontane, Bismarck was without peer.
His Reichstag speeches could be "pure honey."[5] His
speeches to other audiences could be similarly sweet and
nourishing. "I just read Bismarck's speech to the students,
and I think it is magnificent, the crowning act, the essence
of a lifetime, the proverbs of Solomon, only I like it
better."[6]

As a politician, Bismarck was, to Fontane, a virtuoso.[7] As a statesman, he was the master builder; "what Frederick [the Great] did was smaller, and what Napoleon did was more ephemeral."[8] In one half-serious, half-ironic poem, Bismarck is seen as Zeus come to earth to establish order in Germany.[9] The treatment accorded to Bismarck by the successors of Wilhelm I appalled Fontane. He was seldom as sharp in his condemnation of "the proverbial ingratitude of the Hohenzollern" or as extravagant in his praise of the Chancellor as in the spring of 1888, when Bismarck appeared to be in temporary eclipse during the brief reign of Friedrich III, or again some years later, when Wilhelm II publicly depreciated his achievements.[10] And it is a poem by Fontane *"Wo Bismarck liegen soll*—Where Bismarck Should Rest," written in the last year of his life, and on the day of Bismarck's death, which is engraved in the Bismarck Mausoleum in Friedrichsruh:[11]

Nicht in Dom oder Fürstengruft,
Er ruh in Gottes freier Luft
Draussen auf Berg und Halde,
Noch besser: tief, tief im Walde;
Widukind lädt ihn zu sich ein:
"Ein Sachse war er, drum ist er mein,
Im Sachsenwald soll er begraben sein."

Der Leib zerfällt, der Stein zerfällt,
Aber, der Sachsenwald, der hält;
Und kommen nach dreitausend Jahren
Fremde hier des Weges gefahren
Und sehen, geborgen vorm Licht der Sonnen,
Den Waldgrund in Efeu tief eingesponnen
Und staunen der Schönheit und jauchzen froh,
So gebietet einer: "Lärmt nicht so!—
Hier unten liegt Bismarck irgendwo."

Not in cathedral or royal crypt,
He rather should rest in God's free air.
Outdoors, on slope or mountain.
Or better yet: deep, deep in the woods.
Widukind invites him:
"He was a Saxon, hence he is mine
Let the Saxon Forest his burial place be.

Body and stone disintegrate
But the Saxon Forest lasts.
And if, after three thousand years,
Strangers should come passing by
And see, hidden from the light of the sun
The forest floor deep in ivy
And, amazed by this beauty, shout with joy
Someone will command: "Not so much noise!
Bismarck is buried somewhere near."

It is a poem which leaves a later reader with a slight feeling of unease, one reason why only a prose translation has been attempted. It is moving. The sentiments are genuine. Yet it is all too heroic and too grand, for Fontane as well as for Bismarck. And one wonders, too, about the poem's almost pagan note. The man whom it commemorates had taken his Protestant faith seriously indeed, and while there is nothing to indicate that Fontane was a believing Christian, the cult of Widukind and of the Saxon Forest was equally alien to him. Beside, there is the fact that Fontane had often spoken of the living Bismarck in considerably less reverent terms, for he had sensed the Chancellor's weaknesses. Fontane shared his reservations with many Germans of his time, of course, but few expressed their qualms quite as bluntly.[12]

One failing he attacked was the Chancellor's inability to tolerate any political talent other than his own in his vicinity: "only people lacking in any spirit of independence or persons of the second or third rank can serve next to a despot like this."[13] Another criticism, and it was one to which Fontane frequently returned, concerned Bismarck's personal character defects. He was a great statesman, no doubt about it. But "ultimately, what is best in me turns away from him—his nature is not noble—*Ich bin kein Bismarckianer, das Letzte und Beste in mir wendet sich von ihm ab, er ist keine edle Natur.*"[14] Concluding a bitter attack on the Prussian nobility for its lack of generosity and of that spirit of fair play and service which distinguished the British squire, Fontane wrote: "Take Bismarck. Great as he is, and much as I admire him, that which Washington had, and the Elder Pitt, *that* he does not have."[15] "People say," he wrote to Count Phillip Eulenburg, " 'he is a great genius but a small man.' "[16] Whether people were saying just that or not, Fontane was. And he was aware of the extent to which Bismarck's personal shortcomings were corroding his work. Three of Fontane's letters on the subject are worth quoting at some length. Rare are the historians who, with all the advantages of hindsight at their command, have said shrewder things about Bismarck. The first letter, written in the summer of 1893, is addressed to his old friend August von Heyden:

"You ask about Bismarck. My ladies, who read the paper to me, must have let their attention wander. I do not know anything about a speech in Hanover.[17] But I suppose it was like all the others. This eternal pose of orphan boy and fellow honest-as-the-day-is-long is terrible. One must forever recall the giant achievements of his genius if one does not wish to be repelled by his dishonesty, which rests on the crassest of contradictions. He is the most interesting character imaginable. I do not know a more interesting one. But I really am disgusted by this unending tendency to cheat, by this total foxiness.

"If I wish to be inspired, I have to look to other heroes. To subordinate everything to expediency is an appalling tendency in any case, and in his particular one there is so much that is personal and ugly mixed in with it all: the need for applause, the unconditional faith in the justification of every mood and brainstorm of his, and colossal greed. I am delighted, time and again, by the genius which speaks from every one of his sentences; time and again, my reservations go overboard; but then, when I think calmly, the reservations always reappear. There is no field where you can entirely trust him.

"On the other hand (criticism is cheap) his critical remarks always hit the nail on the head: he undoubtedly is right in suggesting that our state of affairs is precarious and that a profound lack of confidence fills the land."[18]

Fontane expanded on the same theme in another letter, written shortly thereafter, in which he found some bitter words, too, about Bismarck's frequent professions of loyalty to the crown:

"Bismarck was the greatest despiser of principles who ever existed, and a 'principle' finally made his fall and defeated him—the same principle which he always carried on his flag and which never influenced his actions. The power of the Hohenzollern monarchy (a well-deserved power) was stronger than his genius and his cheating. He bears the closest resemblance to Schiller's Wallenstein (the historical Wallenstein was different): genius, savior of the state, and sentimental traitor. [Again, Fontane's private comments and his fiction complement each other. "Any successful general is a danger," warns Dubslav von Stechlin, adding: "And others, too, sometimes. Look at the old fellow from the Saxon Forest, our civilian Wallenstein."[19]] Always I, I, and when things go wrong, complaints about ingratitude and a sentimental North German tear. Wherever I see Bismarck as a tool of Divine Prov-

idence, I bow before him. Wherever he is simply himself—country squire and captain of the dike and man out
for his own advantage—I dislike him profoundly."[20]

And in a letter written on the Chancellor's eightieth
birthday, Fontane once more returns to this theme of the
two faces of Otto von Bismarck:

"It is a pity that this day, at least in my eyes, is not
what it might be. And that is, again according to my
feelings, Bismarck's fault. This mixture of superman and
slyboots, of a man who has founded an empire and who
won't pay the taxes on his stables (he thought the city
of Berlin wished both to annoy and to cheat him), of
hero and cry-baby who has never hurt a fly, fills me with
mixed emotions and prevents any pure and bright admiration. Something is lacking in him, the very something
which bestows real greatness. Neumann, the banker across
from me, did not put his flag out either, and arm in arm
with Neumann I challenge my century."[21]

We read Fontane with the disadvantages as well as
with the benefits of hindsight today. We know how
thoroughly Bismarck's heritage has been squandered. We
know that his Reich has vanished and that his work has
turned out to be more, not less, ephemeral than Napoleon's. We may, in consequence, read too much into
Fontane's words and dwell on Bismarck's defects too
long instead of profiting from the lessons of his statesman-
ship. Still, the accuracy of the vision is startling. So
many of the factors that helped to undermine what he
created are there: Bismarck's methods, in the Arnim affair
and beyond ("he is a great genius but a small man");
the unsolved problem of the succession ("only . . . persons
of the second and third rank can serve next to a despot
like him"); the creation of a state that was tailored to his
own measurements rather than those of its citizens ("always I, I, and when things go wrong, complaints about

ingratitude"). None of these defects may have been strong enough to destroy the new Empire of 1871, but Fontane also had some grave doubts and forebodings about the basic strength of that Empire and of its principal component, Prussia.

CHAPTER VI

Prussia

Simplicity, modesty, truth, lack of pretense—that is
where happiness and beauty are.

THEODOR FONTANE to a young writer,
October 24, 1881

How fortunate that we still have a non-Prussian Germany.

THEODOR FONTANE to Wilhelm Hertz, May 27, 1894

FONTANE LOVED HIS NATIVE BRANDENBURG, the core of
Prussia. His *Wanderungen* were meant to achieve for
Brandenburg what Bodmer's poetry was said to have
done for the Swiss Alps: they wished to make a region
which had seemed forbidding and austere exciting and
beautiful. To a very large extent, they succeeded. "Falken-
rohde is one of those laughing villages of which Brandenburg, its reputation notwithstanding, has so many."[1] Just
how many, Fontane indicated in a poem that opens the
third volume of *Wanderungen*:

More smiling villages than one can see
Line this blossoming tapestry:
Linow, Lindow,
Rhinow, Glindow,
Beetz and Gatow,
Dreetz and Flatow,
Bamme, Damme, Kriele, Krielow,
Petzow, Retzow, Ferch by Schwielow,
Zachow, Wachow, and Gross-Behnitz,
Marquardt-Ütz near Wublitz-Schlänitz,
Senzke, Lenzke, and Marzahne,
Lietzow, Tietzow, and Reckahne,

And to end this enchanted dance
Ketzin, Ketzür, and Fehlefanz.

. . .

Beloved homeland, Havelland![2]

No one else has struck so much poetry from the sandy soil of Brandenburg:

Blaue Havel, Grunewald,
Grüss mir alle beide,
Grüss und sag, ich käme bald,
Und die Tegler Heide.[3]

"I happen to be a Prussian," he wrote to a friend, "and I am glad to be one."[4] Prussia might have its failings, "but when you come to the essence of things, what, to use only half a century by way of an example, does the entire history of Schleswig-Holstein amount to when compared with the period of Frederick the Great?"[5] Moreover, he believed in the virtues that—in the ideal at least, but often enough in practice—distinguished the citizen of Brandenburg-Prussia: sobriety, incorruptibility, dedication to duty, honesty, probity.[6] The advice he gave to a young writer dealt with more than literary technique: "Simplicity, modesty, truth, lack of pretense—that is where happiness and beauty are. You must find your way out of the genius-maze."[7] These were the Prussian qualities he continued to love and to uphold, even when they were obliterated from many a critic's view by some less endearing Prussian traits as well as by some of the "genius-maze" that characterized the new Reich. "My ideas about Prussianism," he wrote to one such critic whom he knew and liked, "are very similar to yours, even though I am a sworn partisan of Prussia and Brandenburg. I abhor much in this eternal drill, in these signs posted by the state which fix a man's position for life. On the other hand (and here

I very much disagree with you) it is the true spirit of Prussia—something very different from Prussianism—which has supplied the historical and poetic material to German literature, and its writers too, for the last hundred years. There remains a non- or anti-Prussian portion, but lyric poetry aside, it is not much. Of course I count Lessing as a Prussian, and what could be more Prussian than *Minna von Barnhelm* or *Nathan?*"[8]

"I abhor this eternal drill. . . ." Once again, Fontane was no uncritical lover. He knew Prussia's weaknesses, and it may be instructive to see which ones he singled out for his most vocal attacks.

One was the absence of imagination. The price of Prussian sobriety, he felt, was dullness. Dubslav von Stechlin's sister Adelheid, for instance, is a woman of great common sense and a kind heart besides. "However, what made it difficult, in spite of these excellent traits, to get along with her was the profound prosaicness of her character, the Brandenburgian narrowness, the distrust of everything which so much as touched on the realm of beauty and freedom."[9] Something might be said, of course, for the "profound prosaicness" of Prussia. We live in an age, after all, which has seen too many disastrously imaginative regimes. It is Adelheid von Stechlin herself who puts the case very nicely, on the occasion of advising a young relative to remain in that world to which he belongs, and to marry the daughter of a local squire: "I once heard it said that our Brandenburg was the one country which never produced any saints, but where, on the other hand, no heretics were ever burned either. Look, that is what matters: the middling state of affairs. On that you can build happiness."[10]

Had she eavesdropped, perhaps, on a conversation between the director of an annual Paris art exhibit and President Jules Grévy? "No extraordinary paintings this year, but a good average," said the director as he showed his visitor around. "A good average!" replied the President. "Just what a democracy ought to have."[11]

Whether she had listened in or not, Fontane could not quite bring himself to agree with either Adelheid von Stechlin or the President of France. The whole basis of Prussian life, he thought in his gloomier moments, precluded both happiness and liberal democracy.

The country simply was too poor for either. Why was the Brandenburger such a hard man, someone asks in the *Wanderungen*, "such a mean hard man," and goes on to supply the answer: "Because he does not have anything himself. It's pure starvation. . . . It's pure, yellow sand. And where you have pure, yellow sand, you'll also have pure, yellow envy. No one is happy to see anyone else own anything. And the words 'to give' or 'to help' aren't part of the vocabulary at all. . . . Everything is poor, and poverty has never produced anything good."[12]

It had certainly never produced any true instinct for liberty. Freedom, Fontane thought, might not necessarily flow from property, "but the reverse is correct: no freedom without property. And ten acres of sand are no property."[13] In the Prussian past, the absence of freedom might not have been disastrous, for the rule of law prevailed. "Having a state that centered around the army did not mean that the state was not based on law—*Der Militärstaat schloss den Rechtsstaat nicht aus*."[14] In fact, if one wished to find fault with Old Prussia, thought Fontane, it was not in the absence of impartial laws, but rather in the rigidity of their application.

The incident which to his mind illustrated this the most sharply was the trial of Lieutenant Katte. The story itself forms perhaps one of the best known chapters in the life of Frederick the Great. In 1730, the eighteen-year-old Crown Prince had decided to seek refuge from the terrible temper of his father, Friedrich Wilhelm I, by fleeing abroad. He was aided in his enterprise by a young friend, Lieutenant Katte, who acted from a mixture of motives no later historian can untangle, but in which both a genuine friendship for the prince and the desire to gain the favor of Prussia's future sovereign may have played their parts. In any event, the royal flight ended almost as soon as it began, and what had started as something of a game quickly turned into dead earnest as both Katte and the young prince found themselves facing a court-martial. To Friedrich Wilhelm's violent anger, the court declared the case of Prince Friedrich beyond its judicial competence but sentenced Katte to prison for life. The King's response was to do what in strict legality he was entitled to do: he changed Katte's prison sentence to a death sentence. Nor did he relent and commute the sentence later. As Friedrich was forced to watch, Katte's head fell on November 6, 1730, in the courtyard of the fortress of Küstrin.

Fontane's sympathies in retelling the story are very much on the side of Friedrich Wilhelm I. Katte, he thought, was plainly guilty as charged. He had aided and abetted the Prince's plans for desertion and had prepared his own. He had, in short, committed a capital offense. Besides, Fontane thought that there was true greatness, of a terrifying kind but greatness nonetheless, in Friedrich Wilhelm's instructions to the court to apply the law in all its severity. The King had quoted scripture, reminding the court of Deuteronomy 17:11: "According to the sentence of the law which they shall teach thee, and according to the judgment which they shall tell thee, thou shalt do: thou shalt not decline from the sentence which they shall shew thee, to the right hand, nor to the left." The King also, in justifying the death sentence against Katte, had written that if the court's more lenient penalty should be allowed to stand, he "would be unable to rely on any officer or servant who is bound by duty and oath. For if such things occur once, they can occur more often. But then all culprits would use the pretext of the Katte case and say that since he got off so easily and smoothly, they should be treated in a like manner. H. M. went to school, too, in his youth, and learned the Latin proverb, *'Fiat justitia et pereat mundus.'* Justice shall therefore be done, and Katte . . . be brought from life to death by the sword. When the court-martial informs Katte of the sentence, it shall tell him that H. M. is sorry, but that it is better that he should die than that justice should vanish from the world."

If the King could be criticized, thought Fontane, it was for trading moral roles with the judges of the military court—it should have been the function of the court to apply the letter of the law, and that of the King to show generosity. Instead, Friedrich Wilhelm "thought justice more important than mercy. And that is not the way it should be. Yet if anything can reconcile us to it, it is that he felt this in his own heart. Let us listen to him again: 'When the court-martial informs Katte of the sentence, it shall tell him that H. M. is sorry, but that it is better that he should die than that justice should vanish from the world.' It is a magnificent sentence, which I have never read (and I have read it often) without being moved most profoundly."

We are reluctant to accept Fontane's position. True, some of his feelings have been shared, to a rather remarkable extent, by writers of other nations and ages. Thus Pierre Gaxotte, in his Frederick biography, while taking full account of Friedrich Wilhelm's terrible temper and showing less charity than Fontane toward the King's motives in this particular episode, still makes the similar comment that "there is in this letter a homely grandeur

which is not counterfeit."[15] Granted, but too many un-
answered questions still remain. Had not Friedrich Wilhelm, even in an age and society which did not choose
to make very clear distinctions between judicial and
executive functions, violated the spirit of the law and of
justice by overriding the court's decision? Had he not
perhaps been more interested in finding a scapegoat
rather than justice? After all, the principal figure of the
tragedy was Friedrich, who lived to be king, and not
Katte, who had to die. Had not the more honorable role
been played by the aged President of the Court, Count
von der Schulenburg, who replied to the King's pressure
for the death sentence by saying that, "having thoroughly
contemplated and considered the matter once again, he
was convinced before his conscience that the sentence
would have to remain as it stood, and that it could not
be altered without injury to his conscience, and that it
was beyond his power to do so"?

No matter; whatever our reservations might be, Fontane thought that justice was on Friedrich Wilhelm's
side, and that his decision had been a quintessentially
Prussian one, Prussian justice being "straight justice, al-
beit of a sharp kind." For all its horror, Katte's execution
was the event which showed "the *moral* force on which
this land, this equally hatable and lovable Prussia, is
based."[16]

What had changed in Prussia since the days of Friedrich Wilhelm I was similarly hatable and lovable at one
and the same time. The law had become less harsh; it
also, however, had perhaps become a bit less objective.
What occasionally worried Fontane about the Prussia in
which he lived was increasing police arrogance and the
tendency of the police to place themselves above the
law.[17] His misgivings here were of a fleeting kind, caused
by the repressive measures which followed the failure

of the 1848 Revolution. Prussia basically remained a *Rechtsstaat* to him. Yet the theme of Prussian—if not of police—arrogance is one to which he would return. He thought that the time had come to be less simple in one's purpose and less bullheaded in one's means, legal and otherwise, than Friedrich Wilhelm I had been. One should begin to mend one's manners; the age one lived in called for gentler gestures.

Herr von M., he wrote to his daughter, was quite right in saying that Prussia had become great by taking itself and the world terribly seriously—*"durch sein alles Wichtignehmen."* (Herr von M. was a country squire in whose house Martha Fontane had recently begun working as a governess.) The country was poor; how else was it to amount to anything? Originally, one should recall, "there was little or nothing in the territory between Oder and Elbe, and the two organizing geniuses, Friedrich Wilhelm I and Friedrich II, created real values by means of artificial values, just as financial geniuses have always known how to transform paper values into gold. Both of these kings would pick out a very ordinary and often rude fellow and tell him: 'You are now a treasurer or a tax inspector or a postmaster or even an ambassador.' All four of them, in most cases by far, remained rude and rough and selfish people. But the rank they held, the preferred position they enjoyed, the monetary advantages that were theirs gave them a feeling of social and, in the end, of personal confidence which bore some fruit in the second and third generation. There had meanwhile been created not only a state but, and this impresses me even more, a group of clever and honest and even noble-minded families. All this from 'taking oneself seriously,' all this from the unceasing feeling that a royal postal secretary, a royal rodmaster, a royal clerk were terribly important persons."

But times had changed, and Prussia should change with them. The state was securely established by now, and the insistence on appearances ought to end. It was time for Prussian edges to be blunted. "We are over our roughest period. . . . A lieutenant should only be a lieutenant, and even if he is serving with the Zieten hussars or wears the death's-head on his fur cap, he should forego wishing to be a demi-god or something in any way exceptional. But we are still operating with *false values*. . . . We must begin to operate with *real* qualities now, and to take things for what they *are*, and not for what they *seem* to be."[18] "One more," says a young woman in one of his novels, as she glances at a calling card whose owner has added the line "Lieutenant (Reserve) of the Fifth Dragoons" after his name. "I find it appalling, this eternal lieutenant. There aren't any individuals left."[19]

Yet there should be. "A lieutenant should only be a lieutenant"—it was here, in particular, that one should adopt the customs of the civilized world. The adulation of the soldier, "this eternal drill," had never been attractive to Fontane, and he cited Frederick the Great's famous order of rank—"the oldest privy councillor behind the youngest ensign"—with distaste. He again granted that there might have been some justification for such an attitude in the past: "Prussia was Prussia because of its army, not because of its wealth and agriculture."[20] But the reason no longer held, and Fontane found Prussia's military airs increasingly offensive. "How fortunate we are that we still have a non-Prussian Germany," he told his publisher, and this time there was little irony in his voice. "Oberammergau, Munich, Weimar—those are the places that make one happy. Faced with standing-at-attention, fingers-to-the-trouser-seam, Leist and Wehlan,[21] I get sick. And I am a dyed-in-the-wool Prussian. How do you suppose others will feel?"[22]

He knew how they felt. He knew how many people would have no part of Prussia and would be all too ready to agree with his own occasional observation that "true crudeness—*eigentlicher Knotismus*"—could be studied only in Berlin.[23] Even in one of his theater reviews, he strikes this note of dejection and of warning: "At the bottom of the national soul there still rests the old dislike of us, and we should be careful lest we rouse the old anger by proclaiming from the stage, again and again, the quite untrue news that we are especially fine people. The time may come very soon when the spirit of Berlin and of Brandenburg, which still rules, will urgently need the sympathies of all Germany. And Bismarck is old and Moltke is older."[24]

Prussianism, for all its achievements, for all the terrible grandeur of Friedrich Wilhelm I, in the end rested on "feet of clay."[25] The truly frightening thought was that even these feet might be stronger than those of the new German Reich.

CHAPTER VII

The Reich That Bismarck Built

> ... I would gladly follow him [Wilhelm II]
> on his tightrope walk if only I could see the
> right sort of chalk under his feet and the
> proper balancing-staff in his hands.
>
> THEODOR FONTANE to Georg Friedlaender,
> April 5, 1897

FONTANE REJOICED in the creation of Bismarck's Reich: "Germany has come of age."[1] He thought that Prussia's cultural horizons had been immensely widened by it,[2] and he was happy to see a strong and compact Reich in place of the weak and disjointed states which had been responsible for the nation's political impotence before 1871.[3] "We Germans are on top again," says Major von Stechlin with some satisfaction, adding a reflective "a little too much so."[4]

"A little too much so." The qualification almost strikes us as Stechlin's—and Fontane's—version of the constant *"pourvu que ça dure"* of Napoleon's mother. Essentially, Fontane's faith in the permanency of it all was as fragile as Letizia Bonaparte's had been. The flaws he saw were too numerous: the exaggeration of externals, the apotheosis of the second lieutenant, the weakness of the bourgeoisie, the inadequacy of Germany's leaders, the widespread lack of confidence in the political fortune of the new nation.

All of these criticisms might be found in other sources too, from the *Simplicissimus* to Stefan George to Maximilian Harden. What makes them so impressive in Fontane's case again is that there is more melancholy than contempt in his voice. His criticism comes reluctantly, and his villains as well as his heroes are drawn in more than one dimension. No matter how much his temper might rise, Fontane would not play the role of the caricaturist, polemicist, or Old Testament prophet. No one, he knew, had appointed him *magister Germaniae* or Elijah. No one, of course, had so appointed Harden, but Fontane, who lacked arrogance, was more aware of his limits. The Prussian officers in Fontane's novels, for instance—Captain von Czako in *Der Stechlin* or Lieutenant von Rienäcker in *Irrungen Wirrungen*—are sensitive, intelligent, and soft-spoken people. They are blessed with a sense of humor as well as with a sense of their own shortcomings and are as far removed from the standard *Simplicissimus* or standard American version of the arrogant Prussian officer as today's American is from his caricature in *Krokodil*. All the same, Fontane also could assail the military spirit when it infected the civilian sphere as it too often did in Bismarck's Reich.[5] For his taste, there was far too much in German life that smelled of barracks and parade ground.[6]

"Dynasty, government, nobility, army, scholars—all are honestly convinced that we Germans in particular represent a high culture. I deny it. Agreed, army and police represent culture, too, but culture of a lower order, and the life of a nation and a state which is determined by these two forces is far removed from a truly high stage."[7] As he put it even more cuttingly to his old friend Georg Friedlaender: "Every class, every family, has its definite idol. One may say, however, that there is a total of no more than six idols in Prussia, and the chief idol, the Huitzilopochtli of the Prussian rite, is the second lieutenant, the reserve officer. That's where the body is buried."[8]

In a similar vein, Fontane, while appreciating the virtues of the well ordered life and of certain visible distinctions of rank and position, thought the importance attached to such externals in the Germany of Bismarck

and Wilhelm II altogether ludicrous.[9] "If I were a man
with a social position," he wrote to Friedlaender after he
had been awarded the Hohenzollern *Hausorden* in 1889,
". . . this distinction would have practically no meaning
for me. But in view of the fact that in Germany, and
particularly in Prussia, you count for something only if
you are 'government graded,' such a medal has some real
practical value: people look at you with greater respect
and treat you more decently. So let us bless Gessler, who
'submitted' me."[10]

The object of Fontane's derision was not peculiar to
the new Reich only, of course. It had characterized an
older Germany, too. "The Germans," Mme. de Staël had
noted three quarters of a century earlier, ". . . have as
much need for method in their actions as they have for
independence in their ideas. The French, on the contrary,
treat actions with the freedom of art and ideas with the
slavery of usage. The Germans, who cannot tolerate the
yoke of rules in literature, wish everything in the line
of conduct to be traced out for them in advance. They
do not know how to deal with men, and the less occasion
one gives them in this connection to make independent
decisions, the more pleased they are."[11] But Fontane
might not have been entirely convinced that either
the flight into government approval or the wholesale ac-
ceptance of military values were quite such venerable
and ineradicable features in German life. It was Fontane,
after all, who revived the story of a Prussian who held
these qualities in some contempt, in the story of Johann
Friedrich Adolf von der Marwitz of Friedersdorf, the
Prussian squire who served as a colonel under Frederick
the Great. It may best be told in Fontane's own words:

"He entered the regiment Gendarmes and advanced
step by step. He was a very decent and widely respected
soldier, an elegant and civilized man of the world, a friend

of literature and of the arts. The Great King thought highly of him, particularly as he had most successfully led the regiment Gendarmes through almost the entire Seven Years' War, in place of the regiment's nominal commander, Count Schwerin.

"Thus the year 1760 arrived. The king had not forgotten that it had been Saxon troops who had looted Castle Charlottenburg the previous year. Filled with the desire for revenge, he ordered, immediately upon entering Saxony, the destruction of Castle Hubertusberg—the same castle that was to become famous later because of the peace that would be signed there. The looting officer was to receive the castle's furniture. The order went to our Marwitz, a colonel at the time. Marwitz shook his head. A few days later, at dinner, the king asked him whether Hubertusberg had been looted. 'No,' replied the Colonel. Another half week passed, and the king repeated the question, to receive the same laconic answer. 'Why not?' the king flared up. 'Because this might be proper, if proper it be, for an officer in charge of a battalion of irregulars, but not for the commander of His Majesty's Gendarmes.' The king rose in anger and presented the castle's furniture to Colonel Quintus Icilius, who soon looted every last object.

"During every troop review in the peace that followed, the king was always very much displeased; other officers were preferred to the brave colonel of Gendarmes, and Marwitz submitted his resignation. The king refused it. New insults followed. Marwitz again requested his release from the service. No answer. Thereupon, Johann Friedrich Adolf did not appear for his duties and stayed home for a full year. Now the king became conciliatory and offered him the next vacant regiment. But in vain. His response was that he had served in such a fashion that he did not have to put up with a *passe-droit*; what had happened had happened and no king could undo it. He also submitted his resignation for the third time, and this time it was accepted (1769).

". . . This Johann Friedrich Adolf, or Hubertusberg Marwitz, as we have called him, died in 1781. The church of Friedersdorf preserves his memory with a tombstone on which we read the words: 'Johann Friedrich Adolf [von der Marwitz]. He saw Frederick's heroic years and fought with him in all his wars. He chose disfavor where obedience meant dishonor.' "[12]

We may read too much into the story today. It is, after all, only one among many historical anecdotes Fontane tells in the *Wanderungen*. None of his novels, none of his poems, takes up the theme again, at least not directly. And yet, after one has duly sounded this warning, one may also say that the lessons to be drawn from Marwitz' choice of "disfavor where obedience meant dishonor" are illuminating ones.

The most obvious application, perhaps, is in contemporary Germany. The shortage of *Zivilcourage* clearly contributed its share to the German catastrophe under Hitler. In consequence, the Marwitz incident may well be the most frequently quoted Fontane story in current German literature. Among those retelling it has been the first President of the Federal German Republic, Professor Heuss. In a speech honoring the dead of the July 20 rising against Hitler, he suggested that Marwitz' action was "among those refusals to follow orders which have *historical* importance," and that "if anywhere, Prussia's monument—to use the term as a moral concept—stands in a village church in Brandenburg, in Friedersdorf."[13] Beck and Goerdeler were right, as Marwitz had been; in both instances civil disobedience meant obedience before the moral law. "The brief words of Marwitz' epitaph," wrote a survivor of Stalingrad, "include everything that can be said about obedience, oath, and loyalty."[14]

Another lesson reaches beyond Germany's border. Heuss, South German and Liberal, has used words that compel our attention. If Prussia had less admirable monuments to show, the epitaph at Friedersdorf indeed was the Prussian spirit too. As one reads the vast literature about Hitler and National Socialism, one is astonished how Hitler, *Autrichien déraciné*, managed to make not only his admiring audiences at the Nuremberg party rallies but a sizable number of foreign scholars as well believe that his caricature of a state was Prussian. Yet can there be anything much more antithetical than Friedersdorf and Braunau, than the "No" of a commander of His Majesty's Gendarmes and the murderous obedience of an S.S. colonel of the Adolf Eichmann variety? What a different interlude National Socialism would have been had its basis indeed been Prussian. How many more survivors there would be among us had Frederick's reaction to a rightful defiance of orders (petty, yes, but who was the ultimate winner?) indeed supplied the model for Hitler's reaction in similar instances.

The story may also have its relevance to a matter safely and happily removed from Hitler's state—the still fashionable, apparently endless contemporary American discussion of organization men, conformism, and the like—for it suggests two ingredients without which "nonconformism" is little but a conformist cliché. One is that if the individual is to say "No" to society with any degree of meaning and conviction, he ought first to have a very clear sense of his own values. The other is that nonconformism is impressive only if, as Marwitz was, one is willing to pay the price for one's contrariness.

But these are thoughts that lead too far away from the

present topic. To borrow one of Herr von Briest's favorite phrases, one is entering too large a field, and the paths might be safer were one to return to the nineteenth century and to Fontane.

One of the more ominous aspects of Bismarck's Reich was that there seemed to be too few men like Marwitz and too many like Quintus Icilius among its military. Toward the end of his life, Fontane expressed his concern in a manner somewhat less gentle and circumspect than that which usually characterized his public criticisms. It was a mistake to assume, he wrote in 1898, that Prussia's true progress since the days of Friedrich Wilhelm I had been in the direction of greater individualism, of "*Männerstolz vor Königsthronen.*" Rather, it had been in the direction of Byzantine flattery and lack of character. "True individuals and genuinely courageous people were alive in those days when freedom did not come ready-made and the stick was applied rather freely. Many words and many deeds that refreshed the heart occurred then, words and deeds which would be unthinkable today. In this area even the most courageous people in contemporary life have become shirkers."[15]

Certainly no contemporary equivalent of the Marwitz incident makes its appearance in Fontane's writings. Nineteenth century colonels saved their considerable bravery for battle, with none left to spare when it came to dealing with Frederick the Great's garrulous heir. It was one more reason, if not the principal one, why the army represented a culture "of a lower order." It might not have mattered. Things had changed since the days of Frederick. The army no longer carried the state on its back, or, to be more precise, it no longer needed to carry it. But the grim fact was that no new class had emerged to lead the nation—certainly not the class that was putting its imprint on the state in Britain and France and that one might expect to wield some comparable power in industrializing Germany: the bourgeoisie.

We have noted Fontane's misgivings about the German bourgeoisie before; these did not diminish as he and the Reich grew older.[16] Nor did his confidence in the political acumen of the aristocracy increase. In fact, one is struck more than once by the extravagance with which Fontane at times praised foreigners—Poles, Americans, Britishers—over all Germans. "I always feel good when I breathe the air of England. True, much has improved on this side; true, we are the superiors of our cousins beyond the channel in many an important point. Yet as far as appearances are concerned—*in den Erscheinungsformen*—and unless one wishes to be nothing but a pale and long-haired poet or philosopher, these are crucial—we are still far behind. Deep down we are still clods. . . ."[17]

No matter how powerful the new Reich might be, the German soul, in Fontane's more gloomy moods, remained "small and narrow," and the Reich's citizen "the great clod of world history."[18] The loud patriotism of this sort of citizen repelled him. There were too many patriotic plays on the Berlin stage, he complained in one of his theater reviews. "Let the song of German loyalty and Gallic duplicity come to an end. We have Alsace-Lorraine now and without any particular loss to ourselves can give up one thing in return: our old position as sole lease-holder of morality."[19]

The Byzantinism which filled the air after the accession of Wilhelm II made him even angrier.[20] He had looked on Wilhelm I and Friedrich III without notable enthusiasm but with some respect.[21] The mock-heroic poses struck by Wilhelm II, on the other hand, so appalled and frightened him that he shed much of his Hohenzollern loyalty and by contrast found even the Social Democrats attractive.[22] There were several well-reasoned parts to his indictment of Wilhelm II. The Kaiser's blundering, offensive speeches filled him with "the most awesome fear—*wird mir himmelangst.*"[23] So did the monarch's assertions of *Gottesgnadentum* and absolute power, that "most monstrous of all dogmas, the Stuart concept of the divine right of kings."[24] The lack of any genuine, popular basis of government, which to Fontane at least was becoming more apparent under Wilhelm II than under his two predecessors, similarly disturbed him: ". . . our rights and liberties are ours by courtesy only and can be taken away from us again at any moment. We have everything out of mere pity, and before the power relationship between the old and the new does not change in favor of the new, all our political activities are nothing but words and play acting."[25] Perhaps even more than this, it was the lack of moderation in all things and the substitution of theatrical gestures for statecraft and wisdom which made Fontane fearful of Germany's future.

Dubslav von Stechlin, after some pointed praise for the simplicity and essential humanity of Wilhelm I, goes on to say how that Emperor had been "the last man who still was truly a man. . . . Now we have so-called supermen instead." "Incidentally," the major adds a few moments later, "I say this with all respect. I am no *frondeur.*"[26] Neither was Fontane. Yet the letter which best sums up his attitude toward the emperor almost seems to indicate that he might have been persuaded to become one. It is worth citing at some length. Written to Georg Friedlaender in the spring of 1897, a year before Fontane's death, it may be colored too much by Fontane's by then quite boundless contempt for the nobility ("they should all be boiled alive"); yet it still seems as fair and fresh an appraisal of Wilhelm II as any:

"You mention the speeches given by an exalted tongue, in which so much is said and even more is passed over in silence. I always lose my temper when I read them in my good *Vossin*, although I know myself free from disloyalty and feel gratitude and not just understanding for many of the things desired 'on high.' What I like about the Emperor is the total break with the old. What I do not like about the Emperor is something which contradicts this: the attempt to restore the very old. In some ways, he liberates us from the empty forms and appearances of old Prussia; he makes a break with the rudeness, the smallness, the penny-pinching petty bourgeois ways of the period of 1813. By and large, he has new trousers made instead of patching the old ones. He is most unpetty and dashing [*forsch*], and he thoroughly understands the fact that to be German Emperor is something different from being Margrave of Brandenburg.

"He has a million soldiers and wants to have a million battleships too. He dreams (and let me hold this dream very much to his credit) of humiliating England. Germany is to be on top, in each and every thing. I rather like all this—I won't discuss right now whether it is clever or practical—and I would gladly follow him on his tightrope walk if only I could see the right sort of chalk under his feet and the proper balancing-staff in his hands. But those are things he does not have. What he wants, while it may not be impossible, is vastly dangerous, and his equipment is wrong and his means are insufficient. He thinks he can establish the new with the very old; he wants to establish the modern with arms from the attic. He provides new wine, and since he does not trust the old bottles, he wraps ever heavier cords around them and thinks 'now they will hold.' But they will *not* hold. If you establish new and distant goals for yourself it is not enough to change your flintlock for a percussion gun; you invent some entirely new precision weapons, else there is no point in shooting at all.

"What I suspect the Emperor intends doing cannot be

done with 'weapons' anyway. When I look at all our military efforts I feel as though in the year 1400 all ingenuity had been directed toward making a knight's armor bulletproof. Instead, one finally decided on the only correct solution of throwing that armor away entirely. There will be an inevitable repetition of this: armor must go; other forces must replace it—money, intelligence, enthusiasm. If the Emperor can win these three for his side, he and his fifty million Germans can take up any sort of fight. With tin hats for his grenadiers, with medals, ribbons, and an impoverished country gentry 'which follows its margrave through thick and thin' he *cannot* do it.

"Only popular enthusiasm can perform the miracles he wants, but to awaken it he would have to start slicing the sausage from the other end. The disease of Prussia—and therefore of all of Germany—is the East Elbian nobility. One can visit it as one visits the Egyptian Museum, and one may bow before Ramses and Amenhotep, but to let it govern the country for its own pleasure, in the delusion *this nobility is the country*—that is our misfortune, and as long as this state of affairs lasts, any increase in Germany's power and respect abroad is out of the question. What our Emperor takes to be a *pillar* are only *feet of clay*. We need an entirely new substructure. One is afraid of it, but if one risks nothing he will gain nothing. Cases of states that were ruined by bold reforms demanded by the times are very rare. I know of none. But the reverse shows itself a hundredfold."[27]

Fontane did not think that Wilhelm II had the cure for what ailed Germany any more than Friedrich Wilhelm IV with his dreams of reviving archaic feudal structures had been able to prevent the revolutionary fever of 1848. The parallels between Fontane's evaluation of the two Hohenzollern monarchs—neither in tune with his time, both engaged in a futile search for effective weapons in dusty attics—are indeed striking, and his forebodings that the German patient might be doomed go back to the earliest part of the reign of Wilhelm II. He tried to draw what comfort he could from the thought that even the best diagnostician could not foretell the future—*"es kommt immer ganz anders"*[28]—but as the years passed, even that was no consolation. He was too disconcerted by the Emperor's political eccentricities; what was utterly missing, Fontane became convinced, was the steadfast pursuit of any single political objective. "Our policy resembles that of a knight on a chessboard—only worse, since it is completely unpredictable."[29]

Two things deepened his gloom. One was the Emperor's inability to see the world as it was; what Wilhelm loved was Byzantine flattery, not Prussian facts. To his friend Georg Friedlaender again, Fontane confessed his "infinite loathing for everything that is on top with us today . . . : this narrow-minded, egotistical, crude nobility; this hypocritical, narrow religiosity; this eternal reserve officer; this appalling Byzantinism. Only Bismarck and the Social Democrats give me some pleasure. Neither of them is any good, but at least they don't fawn."[30] The other saddening factor was that despite the parades and outward triumphs of the new Empire, Fontane sensed a profound lack of confidence among many of its citizens. One letter in particular states his views on the matter. It, too, deserves to be quoted at some length. It was written in the summer of 1893 and thus before some of the Emperor's more ominous blunders—there had been no Kruger dispatch yet, no Hun speech, no *Daily Telegraph* interview. Yet, at the height of Germany's success, the letter anticipated the criticisms which most historians made only after the Reich had collapsed: that too much had come, if not too soon, then certainly too quickly, and that the foundations on which Bismarck had built and Wilhelm II had ruled were unsound. Having begun his letter with some sharp words against Bismarck, Fontane went on to say that he did agree with the former Chancellor in this: there was a "deep lack of confidence" in the land.

"The somewhat milder expression 'we don't have the proper confidence in ourselves' might be even more correct. There is open discussion of the collapse of the whole splendor that was built up between 1864 and 1870. Time and again, another hundred thousand men and another hundred million marks are voted, but nobody (even if these additions should continue indefinitely) is at all convinced that our state of affairs is sound. What has been conquered can be lost again. Bavaria may decide to run its own affairs once more. The Rhine province may be lost, and East and West Prussia too, and a Polish state (this is something which I almost think probable before long) may rise again.

"These are not the phantasies of a professional pessimist. They are things which 'once it starts' can take place within a few months, and which exist in the mind of almost every German as possibilities. And now make a rather different test, and compare our state of affairs with that of England at the present time. England, at this moment, stands at the lowest step imaginable, thanks to the follies of the grand old man.[31] Nothing but principles for him. Home rule is a danger, even if nothing should come of it. India is shaky. The mother country has few ties left with Australia and Canada. Russia is gaining the upper hand, and so is France. A situation, at first glance, which is much worse than ours. And yet, what vast difference. Two, three days ago, the great naval maneuvers began in the Irish Sea, and upon my life, I am convinced that there won't be a hundred Englishmen who will not have the feeling when they see this fleet: 'Come what may, the *seas* are still ours, and we'll destroy anyone who'll deny us this dominion. And if our fleet should be lost, we would build another. We have the money for it, and the good will, and the confidence *that it must be so*, *that it cannot be any different.'* We do not have a trace of this confidence. Old Mrs. Wangenheim always told me (putting on her most Catholic face as she did so) 'Prussia-Germany is without promise.' That is right. We are not mentioned in the Old Testament. The British act as though they *had* the promise.

"And now farewell. . . ."[32]

Misgivings not too far removed from Fontane's can be found in Bismarck's mind, too, even before the Chancellor's dislike of Wilhelm II put them there. But in Bismarck's case, the roots of his pessimism were religious. His profound Protestantism reminded him of the dubiousness of all human effort: "Nothing in the world is permanent, neither peace treaties nor laws. They come and go; they change. . . . But we do our duty in the present. Whether it lasts is up to God."[33] In Fontane's case, where evidence of any strong religious convictions is lacking, it was the novelist's sensitivity which made him detect the realities of the present and anticipate the debacle of the future. The black and white Prussian flag which had long flown from Castle Stechlin had become a bit frayed with use. Engelke, the family's old servant, suggests that a stripe be sewn onto it, to make it into the black, white, and red flag of the new Reich. Major Dubslav von Stechlin's answer is: "No. The old black and white will still last—just about—but if you put on something red it will certainly tear."[34]

Perhaps it would be no disaster if it did, thought Fontane as his life was drawing to a close. "All states must regain the courage of not being frightened by defeat. An occasional defeat does not harm a people—neither its honor nor its happiness. On the contrary, the opposite is often true. The defeated nation must only have the strength to rise again on its own resources. In that case, it is happier, richer, more powerful than before."[35]

CHAPTER VIII

The Uses of Hindsight:
Some Conclusions

> Unassailable truths don't exist, or if they do,
> they are dull.
>
> THEODOR FONTANE, *Der Stechlin*

TWO GENERATIONS HAVE PASSED since Fontane wrote his last line. We know the end of the story. We know that the Reich is in pieces. We know, too, how close Europe came to being destroyed along with it. Whether we wish it or not, our knowledge of the present affects our study of the past, affects, at any rate, the kind of questions we are likely to ask about it. The cruellest question, perhaps, that one is moved to ask after having looked at Fontane's political comments is this: How much of a nation was Germany in truth? And there are others, hardly less cruel: How durable was Bismarck's Reich; how solid were its foundations? In fact, how necessary was its creation, in the form it took in 1871? They are questions which should be asked by those who wish Germany well; they should not be left to those who see in German history little but a succession of Hitlers.

Have we not, perhaps, stressed the "inevitability" of German unification too uncritically and for too long? It makes so neat a story: Italy, divided, finally enters upon the path leading to unification under Cavour; Germany, divided, does so under Bismarck. Manifest destiny, economic necessity, the will of the people, the hopes of the poets, the logic of history—there is no shortage of concise and impressive explanations. It may be, we might add in an effort to let minority as well as majority be heard, that there were some, as in Sicily or Bavaria, who held on to the idea of states' rights—"particularists" is our rather derisive name for them—but their day had passed in an age that had embraced a larger cause, in an age, in short, of cultural and political nationalism. Unification, in Germany as in Italy, meant the closing of a volume of the nation's history, a volume that had become too heavy and too long at that.

Was it all that neat and irresistible? Do we indeed open a new volume of Italian history after Cavour, or of German history after the great scene in the Versailles Hall of Mirrors? To what extent was Germany in 1871 truly a nation? It would be foolish to reinterpret history to the point of denying the many ties which held Germans together, in desire as well as in reality; but how tough was the material of which these ties were woven? Let us look across the Vosges Mountains for a moment to see of what material durable ties are made. There could be no doubt whatever, in 1871, that a French nation existed. Old Regime or Revolution, Directory or Napoleon, Restoration or Charter, Second Republic or Louis Napoleon, victory or defeat: *la France est là!* France was a reality. More recently, Raymond Aron, a writer not given to flights of poetic fancy, has summed up and returned the attacks of a small army of contemporary critics of France in one brief phrase: "Eternal France, whose death is feared at any moment."[1]

Eternal or not, both crises and governments in Paris, in Fontane's century at any rate, were ephemeral; France remained. So, in fact, did Prussia or Württemberg. Yet how many Prussians or Swabians would have said *"Deutschland ist eben einfach da?"* And how many, on the other hand, would have said, with Fontane: "We don't have the proper confidence"? Not as Germans, that is, although the black and white of Prussia, or the black and red of Württemberg, or the blue and white of Bavaria might have been good for quite a few more years yet. Where, really, was the German capable of writing the words "Eternal Germany" without sounding either militant or foolish? One's mind rather goes back to one of the epigrams written by Goethe and Schiller during their literary collaboration of the seventeen-nineties: "Becoming a nation, Germans, that hope is deceptive; do instead what you can: develop more freely as men."

> *Zur* Nation *euch zu bilden, ihr hoffet es, Deutsche, vergebens;*
> *Bildet, ihr könnt es, dafür freier zu Menschen euch aus.*

Lack of confidence alone, even if shared by the authors of *Faust* and *Wallenstein,* may not be enough to doom a nation, of course, nor to make its unification undesirable. Confidence can grow. Few nations in the world today are mentioned in the Old Testament. However, too many other weaknesses plagued the Reich of 1871: the personal regimen first of Bismarck and then of Wilhelm II, and the eccentricities of the latter; the preponderance of military over civilian authority and prestige; a shortage of the spirit of Marwitz of Friedersdorf and an excess of that of the second lieutenant (or of the Captain from Köpenick); the obsoleteness of too much of the country's social structure and the unsureness of the new bourgeoisie; the absence of parliamentary responsibility; a foreign policy which, after Bismarck, gained the country little and cost it much; the whole discrepancy between extravagant claims for a place in the sun and a navy second to none on the one hand and the lack of corresponding strength and confidence on the other. Fontane's observations give life to these judgments, the more so since his criticism is tinged with so much reluctance and regret, and balanced by so much awareness of what was *right* with the society in which he lived.

Right and, one supposes, resilient. In contrast to Fontane, we see in Hofmannsthal, for instance, the commentator on a society and a state that have grown even older, and far more fragile, than the *Rosenkavalier's* Marschallin. *"Man wird alt. . . ."*

> *Den Erben lass verschwenden*
> *An Adler, Lamm und Pfau*
> *Das Salböl aus den Händen*
> *Der toten alten Frau!*

Whatever the gesture, it might be the last. Then why not—un-Prussian habit!—squander one's inheritance. One is about to die, gratefully, gracefully.

> *Die Toten, die entgleiten,*
> *Die Wipfel in dem Weiten—*
> *Ihm sind sie wie das Schreiten*
> *Der Tänzerinnen wert!*

> *Er geht wie den kein Walten*
> *Vom Rücken her bedroht.*
> *Er lächelt, wenn die Falten*
> *Des Lebens flüstern: Tod!*

Even without Sarajevo, one feels, Franz Joseph's Austria might not have lived far into the twentieth century. Wilhelmian society, on the other hand, might have; it took four years of bloody warfare, and not internal dissolution, to bring it down. But these are speculations, and treacherous ones, and Herr von Briest was wise to stay away from too large fields.

Let us therefore return to Fontane for a final moment, and to the pleasure he took in what was right about the world around him. His is an approach we might do well to pursue. "Criticism is cheap." It is too easy to be profound about the failings of pre-1914 Germany, since the verdict is in, to the extent that a historical verdict ever is.

What also needs to be said about Fontane's Germany is that life was good and comfortable and decent; that Germans formed no race apart. The family photographs, faded now, do not, after all, lie. It was not only that the clothes were tailored by hand and the houses built to last and the Zeltinger cool and the *Thaler* still a *Thaler*. The moral values were Western values. With all due allowance for the temptations of the flesh, Fontane's citizens and squires were honorable men, believers in the decencies as much as their French or English counterparts. Certainly Fontane's own reaction to such measures as the anti-subversion bill of 1894 was as unequivocal as the attitude of most American intellectuals to the activities of Senator McCarthy. German history was not one great rehearsal for Adolf Hitler. A storm trooper about to bully a Reichstag deputy into silence or to burn a synagogue would have been as much out of place in Fontane's world as in that of Trollope or Henry James. Reading almost any Fontane novel or letter will build up antibodies to even the best and most understanding of books on the theme of Germany's supposed "alienation from the West."[2] And Fontane was too honest a writer to present what did not exist. Fontane, after all, was hardly alone in opposing the antisubversion bill; a very clear majority of Reichstag members agreed with him.

What strikes us then, too, is how interchangeable—for all the differences between Nieplitz and Thames and Seine—is the German family portrait *circa* 1890 with its French or Swiss or Belgian or English counterpart. Too much has been written—understandably so, in the light of Nazi atrocities, but too much nonetheless—about what characteristics set Germans apart. Fontane may serve to remind us once more how much the worlds of *fin de siècle* France and Austria, of Victorian England and Wilhelmian Germany, of squire and *Junker*, of bourgeois and *Bürger* had in common. The differences that existed were fairly subtle ones, differences, more often than not, of degree rather than of quality. Nineteenth century German society and history formed no strange and separate island in the midst of Europe. We might be able to trace the roots of the Reich's collapse back rather far, but for the rise of Hitler, German history will provide only a partial clue.

Besides, we had better be charitable in our judgment of the world now dead. If we ever become too self-righteous, too sweeping and harsh in our criticism, there is always the danger that we might come across a picture of Fontane, smiling.

Notes

Chapter I: THEODOR FONTANE'S LIFE

1. Letter to Paul Schlenther, December 4, 1889, in Otto PNIOWER and Paul SCHLENTHER, eds., *Briefe Theodor Fontanes, Zweite Sammlung* (Berlin, 1910), II, 232.

2. Fontane's two autobiographical volumes, *Meine Kinderjahre* (2nd ed.; Berlin, 1894) and *Von Zwanzig bis Dreissig* (5th ed.; Berlin, 1910) offer memorable pictures of his younger years. Some very good brief accounts of his entire career can be found in the following: the biographical sketch by Edgar GROSS in his edition of *Theodor Fontane, Sämtliche Werke* (Munich, 1959), VIII, 363-66 (which is the best edition of Fontane's novels now available); Paul ALTENBERG, "Theodor Fontane 1819-1898," in Hermann HEIMPEL, Theodor HEUSS, and Benno REIFENBERG, eds., *Die Grossen Deutschen, Deutsche Biographie* (Berlin, 1956-1957), IV, 113-25; Heinrich Wolfgang SEIDEL, *Theodor Fontane* (Stuttgart, 1944), which is relatively untainted by the period in which it appeared; and the biographical introduction to the excellent study by Helga RITSCHER, *Fontane, Seine politische Gedankenwelt* (Göttingen, 1953). Less scholarly, but very readable, is Herbert ROCH, *Fontane, Berlin und das 19. Jahrhundert* (Berlin-Schöneberg, 1962). A special mention should be made of Conrad WANDREY, *Theodor Fontane* (Munich, 1919). Wandrey, after providing a brief account of the essentials of Fontane's career, offers perhaps the most sensitive and intelligent evaluation of Fontane as a writer which we have. His book, besides, has an admirable critical bibliography of works dealing with Fontane. For more specific aspects of Fontane's life, the following are particularly noteworthy: valuable material on Fontane's civil service period is contained in Charlotte JOLLES' clear and factual "Theodor Fontane und die Ära Manteuffel, Ein Jahrzehnt im Dienste der preussischen Regierung," *Forschungen zur Brandenburgischen und Preussischen Geschichte*, XLIX (1937), 57-114, which is identical with the same author's dissertation, "Fontane und die Politik, Ein Beitrag zur Wesensbestimmung Theodor Fontanes," (Teildruck, Bernburg, 1936). For Fontane's historical views, particularly for his views on Prussian history but also for his ideas on the social changes of his day, see Ingeborg SCHRADER, *Das Geschichtsbild Fontanes und seine Bedeutung für die Maszstäbe der Zeitkritik in den Romanen* (Limburg-Lahn, 1950). This is a Göttingen dissertation which is both thorough and entirely objective. The latter quality is all the more impressive as one notes that the dissertation was written between 1941 and 1943. Fontane's politics, in addition to the works by JOLLES and RITSCHER, are stressed in the biography by Mario KRAMMER,

Theodor Fontane (Berlin, 1922). This book, unfortunately, suffers somewhat from the lack of any identification of the many sources cited, and its style might have puzzled Fontane. (*"Wenn wir es als einen Reiz und Vorzug der Denkweise Fontanes empfinden, dass in ihr jener romanische und zugleich nordische Wirklichkeitssinn vorwaltet, der mit hellem Blick die Nebel epigonaler Vorurteile und Illusionen durchdrang, so wird unsere Zeit geneigt sein, einen Mangel an aufbauender Kraft in dieser mehr kritischen Haltung zu betonen. Er ist in den Gegebenheiten nie so weit haftengeblieben, dass er darüber die Aufgaben eines prinzipiell fordernden Politikers vergessen hätte, aber, so viel ist richtig, zu einer Durchbrechung und Auflösung der Realität ist es auf diesem Wege nicht gekommen. . . ."*) For Fontane's contributions to the *Kreuzzeitung*, it is necessary to consult the paper itself, but a selection of his theater reviews for the *Vossische Zeitung* has been edited in book form by Paul SCHLENTHER, *Theodor Fontane, Causerien über Theater* (Berlin, 1905). A recent East German contribution, A. M. UHLMANN, *Theodor Fontane, Sein Leben in Bildern* (Leipzig, 1958), contains some interesting contemporary photographs and documents. For the most recent Fontane bibliography, see the volume published by the Theodor-Fontane-Archiv in Potsdam, *Literatur von und über Theodor Fontane* (Potsdam, 1960). The original version of Fontane's ironic autobiographical poem which serves as the epigraph to this chapter is found in Joseph ETTLINGER, ed., *Aus dem Nachlass von Theodor Fontane* (Berlin, 1908), p. 166.

3. Germaine de STAËL-HOLSTEIN, *De l'Allemagne* (Paris, 1864), p. 65.

4. FONTANE, *Von Zwanzig bis Dreissig*, pp. 346-47. See also his unpublished essay, "Die gesellschaftliche Stellung des Schriftstellers in Deutschland," in FONTANE, "Unveröffentlichte Aufzeichnungen und Briefe," *Sinn und Form*, XIII (1961, Nos. 5-6), 721-23.

Chapter II: FONTANE'S POLITICS

1. Otto von BISMARCK, *Gedanken und Erinnerungen* (Stuttgart, 1905), I, 19.

2. FONTANE, *Von Zwanzig bis Dreissig*, p. 190.

3. *Ibid.*, p. 87.

4. *Ibid.*, pp. 406-33.

5. *Ibid.*, pp. 433-37.

6. Letter to Bernhard von Lepel, October 12, 1848, in Julius PETERSEN, *Theodor Fontane und Bernhard von Lepel, Ein Freundschafts-Briefwechsel* (Munich, 1940), I, 123. For Fontane's political sympathies before and immediately following the revolution, see also most of his *Zeitgedichte* and his Prussian ballads such as "Schill" and "Yorck" in Wolfgang ROST, ed., *Allerlei Gereimtes von Theodor Fontane* (Dresden, 1932), pp. 35-68 and 89-92.

7. Letter to Bernhard von Lepel, April 7, 1849, in PETERSEN, I, 160.

8. FONTANE, *Von Zwanzig bis Dreissig,* p. 112n.

9. Letter to Bernhard von Lepel, April 7, 1849, in PETERSEN, I, 160. See also the draft of the optimistic letter to Georg Günther, written perhaps half a year later, in Friedrich FONTANE and Hermann FRICKE, eds., *Theodor Fontane, Briefe an die Freunde, Letzte Auslese* (Berlin, 1943), I, 30; and the excellent article by Arthur L. DAVIS, "Fontane and the German Revolution of 1848," *Modern Language Notes,* L (1935), 1-9.

10. Letter to Friedrich Fontane, June 16, 1898, in *Theodor Fontane's Briefe an seine Familie* (Berlin, 1905), II, 331. Some but not all of the letters cited from this and other collections have been reprinted in Theodor FONTANE, *Gesammelte Werke,* Jubiläumsausgabe, Second Series (Berlin, 1920), which may be more easily available than the various individual collections.

11. Letter to Georg Friedlaender, March 19, 1895, in Kurt SCHREINERT, ed., *Theodor Fontane, Briefe an Georg Friedlaender* (Heidelberg, 1954), p. 279.

12. FONTANE, *Von Zwanzig bis Dreissig,* pp. 401-04.

13. Theodor FONTANE, *Wanderungen durch die Mark Brandenburg* (Stuttgart, 1919-1920), I, 247.

14. *"Fester Befehl," Gedichte von Theodor Fontane* (Stuttgart, 1912), p. 35.

15. *Ibid.*

16. FONTANE, *Irrungen Wirrungen,* in Edgar GROSS, ed., Th. Fontane, *Sämtliche Werke* (Munich, 1959), III, 171.

17. Letter to Emilie Fontane, August 12, 1883, in *Th. F.'s Briefe an seine Familie,* II, 74. See also the letter to Mathilde von Rohr, May 23, 1888, in PNIOWER and SCHLENTHER, II, 154.

18. Letter to James Morris, January 6, 1898, in PNIOWER and SCHLENTHER, II, 445-46.

19. For Fontane's attitude toward the opposition, see Chapter IV. For a recent sympathetic view of Harden, which yet may leave the reader with a bitter taste about this kind of journalism, see Harry F. YOUNG, *Maximilian Harden, Censor Germaniae* (The Hague, 1959).

20. FONTANE, *Von Zwanzig bis Dreissig,* pp. 304 and 327n.

21. Letter to Hans Hertz, February 20, 1890, in PNIOWER and SCHLENTHER, II, 248. See also the letter to Karl Zöllner, *ibid.,* p. 124.

22. See, for example, *"Bei Torgau," Gedichte,* p. 254, and the perceptive comments of Arthur L. DAVIS, "Theodor Fontane's Relation to German Conservative Forces During the Period 1849-1870," *The Journal of English and Germanic Philology,* XXXV (1936), 262-63.

23. Letter to Emil Dominik, July 25, 1895, in Richard von KEHLER, ed., *Neunundachtzig bisher ungedruckte Briefe und Handschriften von Theodor Fontane* (Berlin, 1936), pp. 108-09.

24. The supposedly favorite flower of Wilhelm I which was worn, in paper replica, by his admirers on the Emperor's birthday.

25. Letter to Wilhelm Hertz, November 24, 1878, in PNIOWER and SCHLENTHER, I, 393.

26. FONTANE, *Wanderungen*, III, 16-17.

27. "Men, do you want to live forever!"

28. FONTANE, *Der Stechlin*, in GROSS, viii, 283.

Chapter III:

THE TWO FACES OF THE PRUSSIAN SQUIRE

1. William L. SHIRER, *The Rise and Fall of the Third Reich, A History of Nazi Germany* (New York, 1960), pp. 93-94.

2. Louis L. SNYDER, *German Nationalism, The Tragedy of a People* (Harrisburg, 1952), pp. 230-31.

3. A. J. P. TAYLOR, *The Course of German History* (New York, 1946), pp. 28-30.

4. See Gordon A. CRAIG, *The Politics of the Prussian Army 1640-1945* (Oxford, 1955), pp. 10-11 and 25-26; and Koppel S. PINSON, *Modern Germany, Its History and Civilization* (New York, 1954), pp. 293-94. Gordon CRAIG also is notable among American historians who have drawn on Fontane for their work; see his *Europe Since 1815* (New York, 1961), p. 382, or *From Bismarck to Adenauer, Aspects of German Statecraft* (Baltimore, 1958), pp. 7 and 45.

5. FONTANE, *Wanderungen*, I, 8-9.

6. FONTANE, *Effi Briest* (Gütersloh, 1950), p. 22.

7. FONTANE, *Irrungen Wirrungen*, in GROSS, III, 131. See also *Wanderungen*, IV, 455-56.

8. Walter KEITEL, ed., *Theodor Fontane, Werke* (Munich, [ca. 1955]) I, 54-55.

9. FONTANE, *Wanderungen*, I, 441.

10. FONTANE, *Der Stechlin*, in GROSS, VIII, 8.

11. *Ibid.*, p. 25.

12. *Ibid.*, p. 11.

13. FONTANE, *Effi Briest*, p. 22.

14. FONTANE, *Der Stechlin*, in GROSS, VIII, 7.

15. *Ibid.*, p. 11.

16. FONTANE, *Irrungen Wirrungen*, in GROSS, III, 208.

17. FONTANE, *Der Stechlin*, in GROSS, VIII, 192.

18. FONTANE, *Wanderungen*, I, 443-46.

19. FONTANE, *Effi Briest*, p. 333.

20. FONTANE, *Irrungen Wirrungen*, in GROSS, III, 120.

21. FONTANE, *Wanderungen*, IV, 455.

22. *Ibid.*, pp. 456-57.

23. FONTANE, *Irrungen Wirrungen*, in GROSS, III, 125-26.

24. FONTANE, *Der Stechlin*, in GROSS, VIII, 39-41 and 107.
25. *Ibid.*, pp. 7-8.
26. See FONTANE, *Von Zwanzig bis Dreissig*, pp. 312-13, and his letter to Henrietta von Merkel, September 20, 1857, in PNIOWER and SCHLENTHER, I, 180.
27. Letter to Emilie Fontane, May 11, 1870, in *Th. F.'s Briefe an seine Familie*, I, 192.
28. See, for example, his letter to Guido Weiss, August 15, 1889, in PNIOWER and SCHLENTHER, II, 208.
29. Letter to Wilhelm Hertz, November 1, 1881, *ibid.*, p. 59.
30. FONTANE, *Wanderungen*, II, 250. The entire section dealing with Marwitz, about whom Fontane finds much that is likable, too, makes rewarding reading. See *ibid.*, pp. 229-52.
31. See FONTANE, *Von Zwanzig bis Dreissig*, pp. 385-86.
32. Letter, January 29, 1878, in Friedrich FONTANE and FRICKE, I, 304-05.
33. FONTANE, *Wanderungen*, IV, 453.
34. Froben, equerry to the Great Elector, died in the battle of Fehr-bellin, according to legend, after changing horses with the monarch in order to save the latter's life.
35. FONTANE, *Effi Briest*, p. 89.
36. Letter, July 12, 1863, in *Th. F.'s Briefe an seine Familie*, I, 130.
37. FONTANE, *Wanderungen*, IV, 453.
38. Letter to Georg Friedlaender, May 14, 1894, in SCHREINERT, pp. 255-56.
39. Letter to Georg Friedlaender, April 12, 1894, *ibid.*, p. 254.
40. FONTANE, *Der Stechlin*, in GROSS, VIII, 253-54.
41. For the parallels between Fontane and Eichendorff mentioned, see "Der Adel und die Revolution" in Gerhard BAUMANN's recent Eichendorff edition, *Neue Gesamtausgabe der Werke und Schriften*, II (Stuttgart, 1957), 1022-44; and the essay by Friedrich HEER, "Die Botschaft eines Lebenden, Joseph Freiherr von Eichendorff," in his *Land im Strom der Zeit* (Vienna, 1958), pp. 168-228.
42. Letter to Emilie Fontane, June 9, 1884, in FONTANE, *Gesammelte Werke*, V, 103. See also FONTANE, *Von Zwanzig bis Dreissig*, p. 327n.

Chapter IV: Workers, Vicars, Bankers

1. Letter to Georg Friedlaender, April 29, 1890, in SCHREINERT, pp. 122-23.
2. This is most clearly shown, perhaps, in Pastor Lorenzen's speech in *Der Stechlin*; GROSS, VIII, 251-52.
3. Letter to Friedrich Stephany, February 23, 1895, in FONTANE, "Unveröffentlichte Autzeichnungen und Briefe," p. 745.

4. Letter to Martha Fontane, August 25, 1891, in *Th. F.'s Briefe an seine Familie*, II, 268-69.

5. FONTANE, *Von Zwanzig bis Dreissig*, p. 7.

6. Germaine de STAËL-HOLSTEIN, *De l'Allemagne*, p. 55.

7. Letter to Martha Fontane, April 18, 1884, in *Th. F.'s Briefe an seine Familie*, II, 90-91.

8. FONTANE, *Wanderungen*, I, 576.

9. Letter to Martha Fontane, April 18, 1884, in *Th. F.'s Briefe an seine Familie*, II, 90.

10. "*Arm oder reich,*" *Gedichte von Th. F.*, p. 83.

11. Fontane's views about the Jews may well be among the most complex and contradictory of all his opinions. They range from admiration and love to misgivings and dislike, but never to programmatic anti-Semitism, which he thought beneath contempt. Having said this much, one is inclined to stop, and the inclination will be followed. No detailed treatment of the topic will be attempted here, partly because it would go beyond the confines of this book, but mainly, perhaps, because his views were too unsystematic, too much subject to changing moods and impressions, so that to sum up in a way would be to falsify. The same holds true for his attitude toward various foreign nationalities—the French or Americans, for instance. The reader who is interested in Fontane's attitude toward Jews is referred to the article by Henry H. REMAK, "Fontane über seine Ballade *Die Jüdin*," *Modern Language Notes*, LIII (April, 1938), 282-87; to the chapter "Fontane Antisemit" in *Erinnerungen an Theodor Fontane, 1819-1898, Aus dem Nachlass seines Freundes und Testamentsvollstreckers Justizrat Paul Meyer* (Berlin, 1936), pp. 13-15; and to the following sources: Friedrich FONTANE and FRICKE, II, 335-36 and 502; Theodor FONTANE, *Briefe an Friedrich Paulsen In 500 gezählten Faksimiledrucken* (Bern, 1949), p. 6; *Th. F.'s Briefe an seine Familie*, II, 128, 285, and 325; FONTANE, *Der Stechlin*, in GROSS, VIII, 300; FONTANE, *Von Zwanzig bis Dreissig*, p. 155; PNIOWER and SCHLENTHER, II, 24, 53, 244-45, and 432; and SCHREINERT, pp. 159-60, 197-98, and 286. For certain similarities between the comments of Fontane in his more acrimonious moods and those of his contemporary, Jacob Burckhardt, see Jacob BURCKHARDT, *Force and Freedom, Reflections on History* (New York, 1943), pp. 46-47.

12. FONTANE, *Wanderungen*, IV, 456-57.

13. Letter to Otto Arendt, December 6, 1888, in PNIOWER and SCHLENTHER, II, 168.

14. Letter to Emilie Zöllner, August 19, 1893, *ibid.*, II, 306-08.

15. See the letter to Emilie Fontane, August 5, 1870, in Friedrich FONTANE, ed., *Theodor Fontane, Heiteres Darüberstehen, Familienbriefe Neue Folge* (Berlin, 1937), p. 120.

16. See FONTANE, *Aus den Tagen der Okkupation, Eine Osterreise*

durch Nordfrankreich und Elsass-Lothringer 1871, in *Gesammelte Werke,* III, *passim;* and the letter to his son Theodor, in *Th. F.'s Briefe an seine Familie,* II, 5.

17. FONTANE, *Aus den Tagen,* in *Gesammelte Werke,* III, 259.

18. Letter to Theodor Fontane, December 13, 1886, in *Th. F.'s Briefe an seine Familie,* II, 144.

19. See the allusions in his letter to Karl Zöllner, July 30, 1874, in PNIOWER and SCHLENTHER, I, 329-30.

20. *Schulthess Europäischer Geschichtskalender,* XXXV (1894) (Munich, 1895), 183-85.

21. Letter to Paul Schlenther, February 24, 1895, in Friedr. FONTANE and FRICKE, II, 552.

22. Letter to August von Heyden, February 27, 1895, *ibid.,* p. 553.

23. *Schulthess' Europaischer Geschichtskalender,* XXXVI (1895), 135-36.

24. Letter to Georg Friedlaender, May 6, 1895, in SCHREINERT, p. 284.

Chapter V:

THE TWO FACES OF OTTO VON BISMARCK

1. Letter to Martha Fontane, March 18, 1884, in *Th. F.'s Briefe an seine Familie,* II, 83. See also the comment in FONTANE, *Von Zwanzig bis Dreissig,* p. 41n.

2. *"Ja, das möcht' ich noch erleben,"* in KEITEL, p. 73.

3. Bismarck, who seldom showed himself in public in civilian clothes, belonged to the Halberstadt cuirassiers, whose uniform collars were indeed a "sulphurous yellow."

4. Letter, March 4, 1894, in "Aus Briefen Fontanes an Maximilian Harden," *Merkur,* X (1956), 1094.

5. Letter to Martha Fontane, March 15, 1888, in *Th. F.'s Briefe an seine Familie,* II, 173.

6. Letter to Gustav Kayssner, April 2, 1895, in Friedr. FONTANE and FRICKE, II, 555.

7. See, for example, the letter to Martha Fontane, March 15, 1888, in *Th. F.'s Briefe an seine Familie,* II, 173.

8. Letter to Martha Fontane, March 14, 1888, *ibid.,* p. 170.

9. "Zeus in Mission," *Gedichte von Th. F.,* pp. 317-20.

10. Letter to Martha Fontane, March 14, 1888, in *Th. F.'s Briefe an seine Familie,* II, 170-71; and letter to Georg Friedlaender, April 6, 1897, in SCHREINERT, p. 311. See also his poem, *"Veränderungen in der Mark,"* (". . . *Gott ist die Gegend runtergekommen"*) written in 1890, in FONTANE, *Romane und Gedichte* (Munich, 1952), pp. 1077-78.

11.   See Willy BRANDL, ed., *Theodor Fontane, Ausgewählte Werke in fünf Bänden* (Stuttgart, 1944), V, 307.

12.   See Richard von KEHLER, pp. 50-51. On the matter of Bismarck's religious convictions, two recent books merit particular attention. One is Leonhard von MURALT, *Bismarcks Verantwortlichkeit* (Göttingen, 1955), pp. 38-140; the other is Gordon A. CRAIG, *From Bismarck to Adenauer*, pp. 3-28.

13.   Letter to Count Phillip Eulenburg, March 12, 1881, in PNIOWER and SCHLENTHER, II, 36-37.

14.   Letter to Georg Friedlaender, April 6, 1897, in SCHREINERT, p. 311.

15.   Letter to Mathilde von Rohr, January 29, 1878, in Friedr. FONTANE and FRICKE, I, 305. See also the letter to Martha Fontane, May 13, 1889, in *Th. F.'s Briefe an seine Familie*, II, 205-08.

16.   Letter, April 23, 1881, in PNIOWER and SCHLENTHER, II, 41.

17.   The ladies' minds may indeed have been elsewhere. On July 29, 1893, while on his way to Kissingen, Bismarck had made a brief speech during a reception given in his honor at Hanover.

18.   Letter to August von Heyden, August 5, 1893, in PNIOWER and SCHLENTHER, II, 303-04.

19.   FONTANE, *Der Stechlin*, in GROSS, VIII, 285.

20.   Letter to Martha Fontane, January 29, 1894, in *Th. F.'s Briefe an seine Familie*, II, 301.

21.   Letter to Martha Fontane, April 1, 1895, in *Th. F.'s Briefe an seine Familie*, II, 308-09.

Chapter VI: PRUSSIA

1.   FONTANE, *Wanderungen*, III, 370.

2.   *Ibid.*, pp. xi-xiii.

3.   *Gedichte von Th. F.*, p. 270.

4.   Letter to Wilhelm Wolfsohn, December 11, 1849, in Wilhelm WOLTERS, ed., *Theodor Fontanes Briefwechsel mit Wilhelm Wolfsohn* (Berlin, 1910), p. 46.

5.   FONTANE, *Von Zwanzig bis Dreissig*, pp. 238-39.

6.   See, for example, WOLTERS, pp. 47-52; and FONTANE, *Wanderungen*, I, 96, II, 209. For a recent German historian's nostalgic and partly personal account of the Prussian virtues, see Hans Joachim SCHOEPS, *Die Ehre Preussens* (Stuttgart, 1951).

7.   "To young X.," October 24, 1881, in PNIOWER and SCHLENTHER, II, 58.

8.   Letter to Leo Berg, July 8, 1888, in Friedr. FONTANE and FRICKE, II, 434-35.

9.   FONTANE, *Der Stechlin*, in GROSS, VIII, 75.

10. *Ibid.*, pp. 148-49.

11. Quoted by Gordon WRIGHT, *France in Modern Times, 1760 to the Present* (Chicago, 1960), p. 297.

12. FONTANE, *Wanderungen*, IV, 20.

13. *Ibid.*, I, 123.

14. WOLTERS, pp. 47-52.

15. Pierre GAXOTTE, *Frederick the Great* (New Haven, 1942), p. 67.

16. FONTANE, *Wanderungen*, II, 302-43.

17. See the article intended for the *Dresdner Zeitung* which Fontane wrote in December 1849 in WOLTERS, pp. 47-57.

18. Letter to Martha Fontane, August 8, 1880, in *Th. F.'s Briefe an seine Familie*, I, 304-05.

19. FONTANE, *L'Adultera* (Berlin, 1925), p. 49.

20. The quotation is from the December 1849 *Dresdner Zeitung* article which the paper refused to print, WOLTERS, p. 50.

21. German colonial officials accused of mistreating African natives.

22. Letter to Wilhelm Hertz, May 27, 1894, PNIOWER and SCHLENTHER, II, 318.

23. FONTANE, *Von Zwanzig bis Dreissig*, p. 44.

24. *Vossische Zeitung*, December 24, 1888, in SCHLENTHER, p. 434.

25. Letter to Friedrich Paulsen, March 14, 1897, in FONTANE, *Briefe an Friedrich Paulsen*, p. 4.

Chapter VII:

THE REICH THAT BISMARCK BUILT

1. Letter to James Morris, March 7, 1898, in PNIOWER and SCHLENTHER, II, 456.

2. Letter to Emilie Fontane, July 18, 1880, in *Th. F.'s Briefe an seine Familie*, I, 299.

3. Letters to James Morris, October 18, 1896, and March 7, 1898, in Friedr. FONTANE and FRICKE, II, 581, and PNIOWER and SCHLENTHER, II, 455-57.

4. FONTANE, *Der Stechlin*, in GROSS, VIII, 55.

5. How correct he was and how the military spirit had indeed got out of bounds after the triumphs of Bismarck's wars has been convincingly described by the two historians who are as expert as anyone in the field: by Gordon CRAIG in the chapter, "The State Within the State," in his *The Politics of the Prussian Army 1640-1945*, pp. 217-54; and by Gerhard RITTER in the chapter on "The 'Militarization' of the German Bourgeoisie," in his *Staatskunst und Kriegshandwerk, Das Problem des "Militarismus" in Deutschland* (Munich, 1960), II, 117-31.

6. See, for instance, the letter to August von Heyden, May 6, 1894, in PNIOWER and SCHLENTHER, II, 317-18.

7. Letter to Gustav Keyssner, May 14, 1898, in Friedr. FONTANE and FRICKE, II, 617.

8. Letter, October 3, 1893, in SCHREINERT, p. 236.

9. See, for instance, the description of Effi's courtesy calls in *Effi Briest*, p. 90.

10. Letter, January 9, 1889, in SCHREINERT, p. 103.

11. De STAËL-HOLSTEIN, *De l'Allemagne*, p. 24.

12. FONTANE, *Wanderungen*, II, 225-27. For the origin of Colonel Quintus Icilius' rather un-Prussian name, and for his subsequent fate, see *ibid.*, IV, 362-66.

13. Theodor HEUSS, "Zur 10. Wiederkehr des 20. Juli," *Die Vollmacht des Gewissens* (Munich, 1956), pp. 532-33.

14. Alexander GRIEBEL, "Stalingrad, oder: Über den Gehorsam und seine Grenzen." *Die Gegenwart*, XI (September 8, 1956), 562-65.

15. FONTANE, *Von Zwanzig bis Dreissig*, p. 321.

16. See, for instance, the letter to Martha Fontane, March 15, 1888, in *Th. F.'s Briefe an seine Familie*, II, 173; or *Der Stechlin*, in GROSS, VIII, 34.

17. Letter to Julius Rodenberg, February 8, 1891, in FONTANE, "Unveröffentlichte Aufzeichnungen und Briefe," pp. 736-37.

18. Letter to Emilie Fontane, July 17, 1880, in *Th. F.'s Briefe an seine Familie*, I, 296-97. Also see the letter to Emilie Fontane of March 10, 1857, *ibid.*, I, 89-90.

19. *Vossische Zeitung*, March 14, 1873, in SCHLENTHER, pp. 433-34. See also the more gently ironic treatment of the same theme in *Effi Briest*, p. 218.

20. Letter to Georg Friedlaender, November 2, 1896, in SCHREINERT, p. 305.

21. See the letters in *Th. F.'s Briefe an seine Familie*, II, 162-65, 179, 181-82, and 191.

22. Letter to Georg Friedlaender, November 2, 1896, in SCHREINERT, p. 305.

23. Letter to James Morris, February 5, 1898, in PNIOWER and SCHLENTHER, II, 452-53.

24. Letter to Friedrich Paulsen, July 13, 1898, in FONTANE, *Briefe an Friedr. Paulsen*, p. 8.

25. Letter to Friedrich Stephany, February 23, 1895, in FONTANE, "Unveröffentlichte Aufzeichnungen und Briefe," p. 725. See also the letter to Georg Friedlaender, April 5, 1897, in SCHREINERT, pp. 309-10.

26. FONTANE, *Der Stechlin*, in GROSS, VIII, 272-73.

27. Letter to Georg Friedlaender, April 5, 1897, in SCHREINERT, pp. 309-10. See also the treatment of the same theme in fictional form in *Der Stechlin*, in GROSS, VIII, 253.

28. Letter to Theodor Fontane, October 19, 1889, in Friedr. FON-TANE, *Heiteres*, p. 235.

29. Letter to James Morris, November 4, 1896, in Friedr. FONTANE and FRICKE, II, 582-83. See also the letter to Morris of March 15, 1897, *ibid.*, p. 596.

30. Letter, November 2, 1896, in SCHREINERT, p. 305.

31. The reference is to Gladstone. The words "grand old man" appear in English in the original.

32. Letter to August von Heyden, August 5, 1893, in PNIOWER and SCHLENTHER, II, 304-06. See also the milder variation on the same theme in FONTANE, *Von Zwanzig bis Dreissig*, p. 49.

33. Quoted in CRAIG, *From Bismarck to Adenauer*, p. 28.

34. FONTANE, *Der Stechlin*, in GROSS, VIII, 12.

35. Letter to James Morris, July 13, 1897, in PNIOWER and SCHLENTHER, II, 427.

Chapter VIII:

THE USES OF HINDSIGHT: SOME CONCLUSIONS

1. Raymond ARON, *France Steadfast and Changing* (Cambridge, Mass., 1960), p. 3.

2. One such unhysterical and useful discussion (though one may disagree with many of the conclusions) is Hans KOHN, *The Mind of Germany, The Education of a Nation* (New York, 1960).

Bibliography

ARON, RAYMOND. *France Steadfast and Changing, The Fourth to the Fifth Republic.* Cambridge, Mass., 1960.

"Aus Briefen Fontanes an Maximilian Harden," *Merkur, Deutsche Zeitschrift für europäisches Denken* (Stuttgart), X (November 1956), 1091-98.

BAUMANN, GERHARD (ed.). *Joseph Freiherr von Eichendorff, Neue Gesamtausgabe der Werke und Schriften in vier Bänden,* Stuttgart, 1957-1958.

BISMARCK, OTTO VON. *Gedanken und Erinnerungen.* 2 vols. (Volks-Ausgabe). Stuttgart, 1905.

BRANDL, WILLY (ed.). *Theodor Fontane, Ausgewählte Werke in fünf Bänden,* vol. V. Stuttgart, 1944.

BURCKHARDT, JACOB. *Force and Freedom, Reflections on History.* New York, 1943.

CRAIG, GORDON A. *Europe Since 1815.* New York, 1961.

———. *From Bismarck to Adenauer: Aspects of German Statecraft.* Baltimore, 1958.

———. *The Politics of the Prussian Army 1640-1945.* Oxford, 1955.

DAVIS, ARTHUR. "Fontane and the German Revolution of 1848," *Modern Language Notes,* L (1935), 1-9.

———. "Fontane as a Prophet of German Political Life," *Modern Language Notes,* XLVIII (1933), 449-52.

———. "Theodor Fontane's Relation to German Conservative Forces During the Period 1849-1870," *The Journal of English and Germanic Philology,* XXXV (1936), 259-70.

EICHENDORFF, JOSEPH FREIHERR VON. *Neue Gesamtausgabe der Werke und Schriften in vier Bänden,* see BAUMANN, ed.

ETTLINGER, JOSEPH (ed.). *Aus dem Nachlass von Theodor Fontane.* Berlin, 1908.

FONTANE, FRIEDRICH (ed.). *Theodor Fontane, Heiteres Darüberstehen, Familienbriefe Neue Folge.* Berlin, 1937.

———, and HERMANN FRICKE (eds.). *Theodor Fontane, Briefe an die Freunde, Letzte Auslese.* Berlin, 1943.

FONTANE, THEODOR. *Allerlei Gereimtes,* see ROST, ed.

———. *Ausgewählte Werke,* see BRANDL, ed.

———. *Aus dem Nachlass von Theodor Fontane,* see ETTLINGER, ed.

———. *Aus den Tagen der Okkupation, Eine Osterreise durch Nordfrankreich und Elsass-Lothringer 1871,* in *Gesammelte Werke.*

———. *Briefe an die Freunde, Letzte Auslese,* see FRIEDRICH FONTANE and FRICKE, eds.

97

————. *Briefe an Friedrich Paulsen, In 500 gezählten Faksimiledrucken.* Bern, 1949.

————. *Briefe an Georg Friedlaender,* see SCHREINERT, ed.

————. *Briefe Theodor Fontane, Zweite Sammlung,* see PNIOWER and SCHLENTHER, eds.

————. *Causerien über Theater,* see SCHLENTHER, ed.

————. *Effi Briest.* Gütersloh, 1950.

————. *Gedichte von Theodor Fontane.* Siebzehnte Auflage. Stuttgart, 1912.

————. *Gesammelte Werke.* Jubiläumsausgabe. Zweite Reihe in fünf Bänden. Berlin, 1920.

————. *Heiteres Darüberstehen, Familienbriefe Neue Folge,* see FRIEDRICH FONTANE, ed.

————. *L'Adultera.* Berlin, 1925.

————. *Meine Kinderjahre, Autobiographischer Roman.* Second edition, Berlin, 1894.

————. *Romane und Gedichte.* (Mit einen Nachwort von Rudolf Pechel.) Munich, 1952.

————. *Sämtliche Werke,* see EDGAR GROSS, ed.

————. *Schriften zur Literatur.* [East] Berlin, 1960.

————. "Unveröffentlichte Aufzeichnungen und Briefe," *Sinn und Form, Beiträge zur Literatur,* XIII (1961, No. 5/6), 704-49.

————. *Von Zwanzig bis Dreissig, Autobiographisches.* Fifth edition. Berlin, 1910.

————. *Wanderungen durch die Mark Brandenburg.* 4 vols. Stuttgart, 1919-1920.

————. *Werke,* see WALTER KEITEL, ed.

Theodor Fontane's Briefe an seine Familie. 2 vols. Berlin, 1905.

FRICKE, HERMANN. *Emilie Fontane. Mit unveröffentlichten Gedichten und Briefen von Theodor und Emilie Fontane.* Rathenow, 1937.

GAXOTTE, PIERRE. *Frederick the Great.* Translated by R. A. Bell. New Haven, 1942.

GRIEBEL, ALEXANDER. "Stalingrad, oder: Über den Gehorsam und seine Grenzen," *Die Gegenwart,* XI (September 8, 1956), 562-65.

GROSS, EDGAR (ed.). *Theodor Fontane, Sämtliche Werke.* 8 vols. Munich, 1959.

HEER, FRIEDRICH. *Land im Strom der Zeit, Österreich gestern, heute, morgen.* Vienna, 1958.

HEIMPEL, HERMANN, THEODOR HEUSS, and BENNO REIFEN-BERG (eds.). *Die Grossen Deutschen, Deutsche Biographie.* 5 vols. Berlin, 1956-1957.

JOLLES, CHARLOTTE. *Fontane und die Politik, Ein Beitrag zur Wesensbestimmung Theodor Fontanes.* Teildruck. Inaugural-Dissertation. Bernburg, 1936.

————. "Theodor Fontane und die Ära Manteuffel. Ein Jahrzehnt im

Dienste der Preussischen Regierung," *Forschungen zur Branden-burgischen und Preussischen Geschichte*, XLIX (1937), 57-114.

KEHLER, RICHARD VON. *Neunundachtzig bisher ungedruckte Briefe und Handschriften von Theodor Fontane*. Berlin, 1936.

KEITEL, WALTER (ed.). *Theodor Fontane, Werke*, vol. I. Munich, [*ca.* 1955].

KOHN, HANS. *The Mind of Germany, The Education of a Nation*. New York, 1960.

KRAMMER, MARIO. *Theodor Fontane*. Berlin, 1922.

Literatur von und über Theodor Fontane. (Brandenburgische Landes-und Hochschulbibliothek, Theodor-Fontane-Archiv.) Potsdam, 1960.

[MEYER, PAUL.] *Erinnerungen an Theodor Fontane, 1819-1898, Aus dem Nachlass seines Freundes und Testamentsvollstreckers Justizrat Paul Meyer*. Berlin, 1936.

MURALT, LEONHARD VON. *Bismarcks Verantwortlichkeit*. (Göttinger Bausteine zur Geschichtswissenschaft, vol. 20.) Göttingen, 1955.

PETERSEN, JULIUS. *Theodor Fontane und Bernhard von Lepel, Ein Freundschafts-Briefwechsel*. 2 vols. Munich, 1940.

PINSON, KOPPEL S. *Modern Germany, Its History and Civilization*. New York, 1954.

PNIOWER, OTTO, and PAUL SCHLENTHER (eds.). *Briefe Theodor Fontanes, Zweite Sammlung*. 2 vols. Berlin, 1910.

REMAK, HENRY H. "Fontane über seine Ballade *Die Jüdin*," *Modern Language Notes*, LIII (April, 1938), 282-87.

RITSCHER, HELGA. *Fontane, Seine politische Gedankenwelt*. (Göttinger Bausteine zur Geschichtswissenschaft, vol. 8.) Göttingen, 1953.

RITTER, GERHARD. *Staatskunst und Kriegshandwerk, Das Problem des "Militarismus" in Deutschland*. 2 vols. Munich, 1954-1960.

ROCH, HERBERT. *Fontane, Berlin und das 19. Jahrhundert*. Berlin-Schöneberg, 1962.

ROST, WOLFGANG (ed.). *Allerlei Gereimtes von Theodor Fontane*. Dresden, 1932.

SCHLENTHER, PAUL (ed.). *Theodor Fontane, Causerien über Thea-ter*. Berlin, 1905.

SCHOEPS, HANS JOACHIM. *Die Ehre Preussens*. Stuttgart, 1951.

SCHRADER, INGEBORG. *Das Geschichtsbild Fontanes und seine Bedeutung für die Maszstäbe der Zeitkritik in den Romanen*. Limburg-Lahn, 1950.

SCHREINERT, KURT (ed.). *Theodor Fontane, Briefe an Georg Fried-laender*. Heidelberg, 1954.

Schulthess Europäischer Geschichtskalender, vols. XXXIV to XXXVII (1893-1895). Munich, 1894-1896.

SEIDEL, HEINRICH WOLFGANG. *Theodor Fontane*. (Die Dichter der Deutschen. Herausgegeben von Kläre Buchmann unter Mitwirkung der Deutschen Akademie.) Stuttgart, 1944.

SHIRER, WILLIAM L. *The Rise and Fall of the Third Reich, A History of Nazi Germany.* New York, 1960.

SNYDER, LOUIS L. *German Nationalism; The Tragedy of a People, Extremism Contra Liberalism in Modern German History.* Harrisburg, 1952.

STAËL-HOLSTEIN, GERMAINE DE. *De l'Allemagne.* Paris, 1864.

TAYLOR, A. J. P. *The Course of German History, A Survey of the Development of Germany Since 1815.* New York, 1946.

UHLMANN, A. M. *Theodor Fontane, Sein Leben in Bildern.* Leipzig, 1958.

Die Vollmacht des Gewissens. (Herausgegeben von der Europäischen Publikation e. V.) Munich, 1956.

WANDREY, CONRAD. *Theodor Fontane.* Munich, 1919.

WOLTERS, WILHELM (ed.). *Theodor Fontanes Briefwechsel mit Wilhelm Wolfsohn.* Berlin, 1912.

WRIGHT, GORDON. *France in Modern Times, 1760 to the Present.* Chicago, 1960.

YOUNG, HARRY F. *Maximilian Harden, Censor Germaniae: The Critic in Opposition from Bismarck to the Rise of Nazism.* (International Scholars Forum, vol. VIII.) The Hague, 1959.

Index